QUICK QUII

MINIATURES

Darlene Zimmerman

Published by

krause publications

The World's Largest Hobby & Collectibles Publisher

Please call or write for our free catalog of publications. Our toll-free number to place an order or obtain a free catalog is 800-258-0929 or please use our regular business telephone 715-445-2214 for editorial comment and further information.

Library of Congress Catalog Number 2001086341
ISBN: 0-87349-239-0

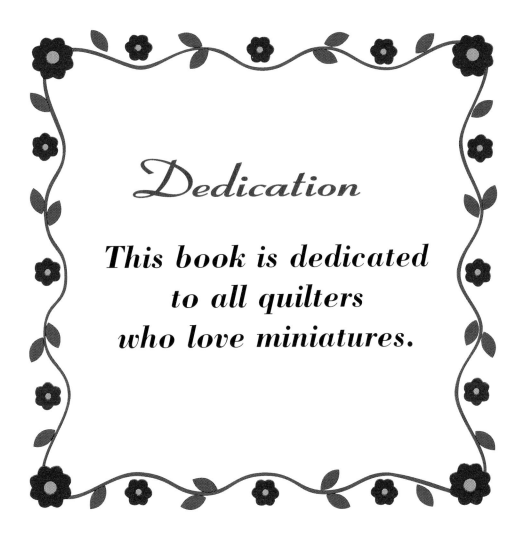

Dedication

**This book is dedicated
to all quilters
who love miniatures.**

Acknowledgments

My heartfelt thanks go out to:
My family, for their assistance and patience in the development of this book.
My son, Don, for his help in editing.
My quilting friends, for their honest critiques and encouragement.
Bernina of America, for the loan of a sewing machine.
Hobbs Bonded Fibers and Fairfield Corp., for its generosity in supplying batting for the projects.
Lisa Kirchoff for the graphics.

Contents

Foreword

Today we have the luxury of making quilts simply because we enjoy the process and love having them in our homes, and not as a necessity for keeping our families warm. In our increasingly mechanized and disposable world, we enjoy working with our hands to create works of art. This labor of love produces an heirloom of lasting value—a quilt. Whether one is a quilt enthusiast, a collector, a traditional quilter, or an artist who works with textiles in the quilt format, all are united by a love of fabrics, colors, and textures.

In today's marketplace, we are overwhelmed by the myriad choices in fabrics, tools, techniques and ideas. Quilters everywhere wail, "How can I possibly make all the quilts I would like to make in my lifetime?" Some of us believe quilting goes on in heaven, but you may find making miniature quilts is instant gratification here on earth. You can usually cut, piece, quilt, and bind a miniature quilt in a day's time. It's exciting to see a project finished so quickly!

Making miniatures allows experimentation with colors and fabrics you wouldn't dare use in a large quilt, and provides the opportunity to try out new settings or border treatments. You may wish to make a miniature as a welcome break from a larger project that has become tedious. Consider making a favorite large quilt or an antique quilt in miniature, or experimenting with a new design or technique without a large investment in time or fabric. For me, and possibly for you as well, the best reason of all for making miniatures is to experience the joy of creating something beautiful.

– Darlene

The purpose of this book is to guide you through the process of creating miniatures, as enjoyably and simply as possible. Using the techniques and tips in this book, quilters of all skill levels should be able to make miniatures. If you're apprehensive about making tiny miniatures, I suggest you start with the larger sizes also presented in this book until you are comfortable with the tools and techniques.

Making miniatures is not difficult; one just needs to adjust to the scale and develop accuracy. Accuracy is the whole secret to making miniatures. You need to be accurate in every step; you must cut accurately and sew accurately. The accuracy that you develop making miniatures is a skill that carries over into your other quiltmaking.

CHOOSING FABRICS

Choosing fabric for miniatures is similar to choosing fabrics for a large project. Of course, you want to use 100-percent cotton fabric—but take a closer look at your fabric. Even among first-quality quilting cottons, there is a wide variance in weave and in the "feel" of the cotton. Some are loosely woven, many ravel more than they should, others are very soft and stretchy, and some are stiff with sizing. You need to be extra careful about your fabric choices. What to use? Let common sense prevail. If a fabric is soft, stretchy, loosely woven or ravels excessively, it is going to present problems in piecing for both a large quilt and a small quilt. However, fabric problems are magnified when making a miniature. You need to be extra careful about your fabric choices. If you absolutely must use a fabric that is less than perfect, spray starch can work miracles. A stiff fabric can make your work much easier. Spray starch and iron the fabric (perhaps several times) before cutting. You may find this so helpful you'll decide to spray starch all your fabrics before using them, which helps you to be more accurate in both cutting and piecing. The entire little quilt can be washed later to remove the starch.

The scale of the prints also needs to be considered. You need to look for small scale prints, but don't automatically eliminate larger prints. If you have a large all-over diffuse design, it may look wonderful cut up. Make yourself a "window"—a 1"-square cut out of the center of a larger square of cardboard. Place this "window" on the fabric and move it around to see what it would look like in small pieces. Of course you lose the all-over design, but what does it look like in small images? Does it look like a solid fabric in areas between the design motif? Does the design look like a part of the whole? It should be interesting enough to stand alone.

When choosing fabrics for a project, think contrast. The contrast needs to be stronger in miniature quilts than in a big project. In a large quilt, subtle color changes can be very pleasing. In a miniature, the same colors will simply bleed together for disappointing results. Pin up 1" swatches of fabric and stand back a few feet to see how they will look together.

ORGANIZING YOUR FABRICS

Our quilting fabrics do seem to accumulate, don't they? We need to find a way to organize and store our fabric so we can find what we need for a particular project. Before you store or use any fabric, however, you should pre-wash it. Then, if a fabric is going to shrink or bleed, it will do so now, before it ruins your quilt. Wash your fabrics by hand or by machine (gentle cycle) in warm water, and dry until almost dry. Iron immediately. If you store only the fabric that has been prewashed in your closet, then you'll be prepared when inspiration strikes or when you are ready to start a new project or make a quilt which utilizes your "leftovers."

A closet with many shelves will allow you to organize your fabrics by color. A closet protects fabrics from fading due to exposure to light and dust (assuming you can close the door!) The shelves allow you to view your fabrics at a glance. Then, when you need a green fabric, you can simply go to the stack of greens and choose the fabric best suited for that project.

After finishing a project, we always seem to have "leftovers," which can be utilized in "scrappy" quilts or miniatures. I save any piece 1" or larger.

Again, to be usable, the fabrics need to be organized. I keep any larger pieces (2" strips or larger) with my general fabric stacks. To store the smaller pieces, I purchased inexpensive, clear plastic stacking drawers that fit right on the closet shelves. I have one drawer for each color or color family. When I need just a 2" square of red, I can find one quickly. It's great to have these small scraps readily available when making miniature scrap quilts or fusible picture quilts.

CUTTING

Accuracy is the key element here. How can the pieces fit properly unless they are cut accurately? Here are a few tips to make your cutting more accurate:

1. Work in good light. You need to be able to see exactly what you are doing. Don't work in a shadow, in dim light, or without glasses if you need them. Whenever possible, work in natural daylight.

2. Only cut two layers of fabric at a time. Yes, you can save a little time by cutting more layers, but you'll lose time and be frustrated when your pieces don't fit together properly.

3. Keep your tools from slipping. You can buy various items to apply to your tools to prevent slippage. Even a 1" square of masking tape will help.

4. Use a sharp rotary cutter. Do yourself a favor and put a new blade in your cutter if it's dull. A new blade will cut more easily and cleaner than a dull blade.

5. When cutting, try to line up the fabric edge on the center of the marking line on your tool, rather than on one side or the other of the line, and be as consistent as possible. For example, when cutting 1" strips of fabric, if you always line up the fabric just *outside* the 1" marking, but for one cut you line up the fabric on the *inside* of the 1" mark, you end up with two slightly different width strips. By aiming for the *center* of the line every time, you will be the most accurate.

SEWING

In making miniatures, I have experimented with sewing both 1/8" and 1/4" seams, and have decided to use only 1/4" seams. I found the 1/8" seams were very difficult to sew accurately because there is no 1/8" marking or foot to use as a guide, and there is a great deal of distortion wherever seams intersect. Also, when I tried to quilt blocks with 1/8" seams, the seams began to ravel and pull apart—a real disaster! With 1/4" seams, the pieces start out much larger, the blocks are easier to draft, and you won't experience distortion when crossing seam intersections. I do **not** trim the seams down later, since it is both difficult and unnecessary, and we don't wish to have the seams pull apart while quilting. Instead, try to distribute the seams as evenly as possible across the back.

How can we teach our sewing machines to sew an accurate 1/4" seam? What good will it do to cut carefully and accurately when your sewing machine doesn't follow through with a consistent and accurate 1/4" seam? Here are a few tips for training the most ornery sewing machine:

1. Have your sewing machine in good working order. I know this sounds obvious, but in the classes I teach, I see many machines that are not sewing properly because of lack of maintenance, a dull needle, or need of a tension adjustment.

2. Use an accurate 1/4" foot (available from most sewing-machine manufacturers) or an accurate guide. To find exactly where that 1/4" seam is on your machine, place one of your acrylic rulers under the needle, with the needle down on the 1/4" mark. Lower the presser foot, and you will be able to see exactly where that 1/4" falls on your machine. Don't guess or assume you are sewing a 1/4" seam—make sure! Mark the 1/4" if the foot you are using isn't exactly 1/4" wide.

3. You will want to adjust to a shorter stitch length, about 12 stitches to the inch. You should still be able to rip out stitches, but smaller stitches help keep the seams together at the edges.

4. Try a smaller needle, or at least put in a new needle if you have been using the same needle for a while. A dull needle tends to push the fabric down into the throat plate.

5. A single-hole throat plate can prevent the fabric from being pushed down into the machine. It is something nice to have, but not strictly necessary.

6. Chain-sew whenever possible, or feed in a scrap of fabric at the beginning and end of each chain or piece you are sewing. To chain-sew, have the units stacked to the left of your sewing machine and simply feed one unit after another through the machine without lifting the pressure foot or breaking the thread. This saves time, thread, and prevents your quilt pieces from being chewed up by the wild feed dogs.

UNSEWING

We aren't perfect, so, unfortunately, mistakes happen or sometimes pieces don't fit together properly. Keep a seam ripper (or better yet, several) handy for these emergencies. Unsewing ("ripping" is such an ugly word) is never much fun, but when your seams are only 1" long, it isn't so bad. When something doesn't fit together nicely, take a moment to analyze why. Is the piece cut the wrong size? Was the seam too narrow? Too wide? You'll never regret having fixed what was wrong in your quilt, but you may regret NOT fixing a mistake that jumps out at you when the quilt is finished.

(***NOTE:*** An option to unsewing is to simply throw away the defective pieces, cut new ones, and start again. Because we are using such small amounts of fabrics, you can tell your conscience you aren't wasting very much. I often make one or two extra triangle squares so I can throw away any that aren't quite perfect.)

Everyone has their own "comfort level" when it comes to mistakes. Don't feel your work has to be 100-percent perfect to be acceptable. After all, we are making folk art, not something stamped out of a machine. On the other hand, we should strive to do our personal best, and to improve with each quilt we make, so we can be proud of our work—not apolo-

getic—no matter what our experience level.

A personal rule I follow: only rip something out three times. If you haven't fixed it by the third try, it isn't going to be fixed and the fabric is suffering. It will just have to be your "humility block."

PRESSING

Pressing is a very important element in all quilt making, whether miniatures or larger quilts. It is always important to press seams before adding another piece to a unit. It isn't enough to just touch the seams with an iron. Press on the right side, open the seam carefully with the iron, and watch that the seam is pressed properly, without distorting the unit.

The direction in which you press your seams is very important in making miniatures. You will have a large number of seam allowances in a very small space, so they need to be distributed as evenly as possible. Follow the pressing directions given in the patterns.

Use a dry iron when pressing small units. This will save your fingers from nasty steam burns and prevent distortion of the units. When a block or an entire quilt top is finished, it is a good idea to use steam and the weight of the iron (rather than moving the iron back and forth) to "set" the quilt.

Try "stack-pressing" your small units for ease of pressing and handling. Stack-pressing is a neat, efficient way to press small units such as triangle

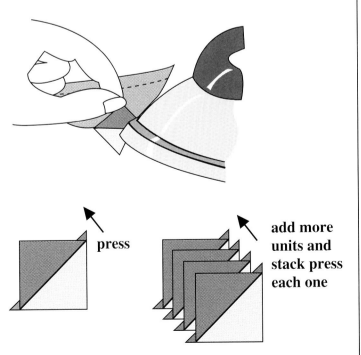

press

add more units and stack press each one

squares or flying geese. Simply place all units to be pressed by your left hand, dark side up. Press the first seam toward the darker unit. Now, with your left hand, pick up the next unit to be pressed and lay it over the first one, off-setting the seam allowance as shown. Press with your right hand. Continue in this manner until the stack becomes too thick. (Reverse this procedure if you are left-handed.) Then, you can pick up the stack of pressed pieces and clip the dog-ears quickly and efficiently. Clip your dog-ears each time you finish a unit. If they are left on, they will get in the way and add unwanted bulk to the quilt top.

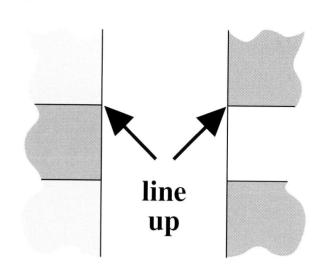

line up

▦ BLOCK ASSEMBLY

Units and blocks are assembled the same way we would assemble them for larger quilts. When joining two units with seam allowances that need to match, have the seams alternate. Place a pin vertically to the seam line where the seams intersect. Pull this pin out as you come to it. It is also helpful to have the seam on top pointing away from you as you sew. The natural action of the sewing machine as it sews over the seams will lock the seams together.

▦ QUILT ASSEMBLY

When assembling a large quilt, we often set our pieced blocks directly next to each other. Look for alternate settings for miniatures because it is difficult to match so many seam allowances. It is much easier to put sashings between blocks than to join the blocks directly. You may choose to square up each block, or you can take up discrepancies in the sashings.

▦ BORDERS

The border or borders for a miniature quilt should act as a frame. After all, miniature quilts are usually hung like a picture. To ensure your quilt is "square," measure through the middle of the quilt and cut the borders to fit the quilt.

A "no-math" approach to cutting borders simplifies the process, and makes it foolproof! Lay your quilt out on a flat surface. Take the strip you are using for your border and use it to "measure" the width or length of the quilt. Match the end of the strip to one edge of the quilt, smooth out the remainder of the strip across the quilt top, and trim it off at the opposite edge. Cut another border the exact same length. They will fit exactly right.

I often use a 1" strip (including the seam allowance) for an inside border or for sashings, which finishes to 1/2". From my friends in North Dakota, I learned to sew an even narrower border (1/4" finished). Begin by cutting a 3/4" strip; sew the first 1/4" seam and then press the seam toward the body of the quilt. Then run the left side of the 1/4" presser foot up

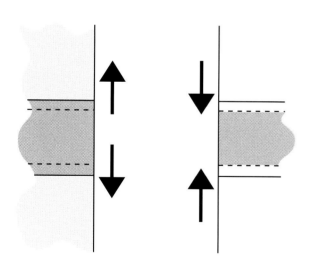

alternate seam allowances between pieces being sewn together

against the seam line, using the previous stitching line as your guide for the presser foot, rather than the edge of the fabric. This will give you an exact 1/4" border.

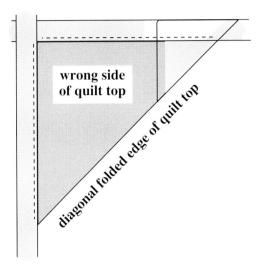

wrong side of quilt top

diagonal folded edge of quilt top

MITERED BORDER

1. Sew the borders to all sides of the quilt, allowing several extra inches for the borders to extend beyond the edges of the quilt and overlapping each other. *Stitch only to within a 1/4" of the corner, stop, and backstitch.* Press the seams toward the quilt.
2. Fold the quilt on the diagonal, right sides together, matching raw edges, and having the borders extending outward.
3. Lay Companion Angle (or a ruler) on your quilt, with the longest edge on the diagonal fold, and the side of the tool aligned with the raw edges of the borders. Draw a line from the diagonal fold to the edge of the borders.
4. Pin the borders together along this line. Stitch on this line, backstitching at the inside corner.
5. Check the seam on the right side. If it is properly sewn, trim the seam to 1/4", and press open.
6. Repeat on all four corners.

BATTING

Over the years, I have experimented with different types of battings to find the one most suitable for miniatures. Without endorsing any one product or company, I would like to make some recommendations.

Polyester battings

Polyester battings usually look puffier than cotton battings. Some polyester battings can be pulled apart, or divided into two layers. Often this half-thickness is thin enough to use for a miniature. There is also a polyester batting designed for garment use. It doesn't beard and has some loft to show off the quilting, but isn't as firm or heavy as the cotton batting. It is quite flat when it comes out of the package, but after I cut it to size and take the batting to the ironing board, where the steam from the iron raises the loft, it is just right to use in a miniature quilt.

Cotton battings

Cotton battings are also a nice choice for a little quilt or wall-hanging. Cotton will have more "body" than polyester, and doesn't beard.

MARKING

Miniature quilts do not need much quilting, but any decorative quilting, such as designs in alternate blocks or borders, needs to be marked before assembling the quilt sandwich. My favorite marking tools are a white chalk marker for dark fabrics and a silver pencil for light fabrics. If I am marking an intricate quilting design on a very light fabric, I may choose to use a blue washout pen, soaking the entire quilt in cold water (NO DETERGENT) after I finish quilting.

Whichever design you choose, keep in mind the scale of the quilt. Many small designs are available in plastic stencils. You may also find small design elements in the stencils you already have. Try to keep the quilting designs *simple*. Elaborate designs on a small scale don't show up very well.

BASTING

If your quilt is 12" square or less, you probably don't need to stretch it for basting. Simply sandwich the layers and either thread or pin baste. For a quilt larger than 12", I recommend stretching and taping down the backing, laying the batting over the top, and stretching and taping the top down. Don't skimp on the basting! You may find it easier to quilt a miniature without a hoop or frame of any type.

QUILTING

On a miniature quilt, one needs to consider the quilting very carefully. Remember, there are a lot of seams on the back side, and it is never fun to quilt through four or more layers of fabrics plus batting. Whenever possible, avoid the seams. If you do find yourself quilting through many thicknesses, you may need to stab stitch (one stitch at a time).

Miniature quilts do not call for large amounts of quilting, but the quilting should be done with care and compliment the piecing. Quilting in the ditch around each block and to define each border is often enough. If you have open areas for quilting or wish to quilt a design in the border, keep the design simple and your stitches small. It is not attractive for a small quilt to have nicely pieced blocks with large, irregular quilting stitches.

Machine quilting is a nice option, if it is done well. Use matching thread so it blends in, and again keep the quilting to a minimum. Stitching in the ditch or a small meander in open areas is usually all you need.

❖ BINDING

Before binding, baste the three layers together less than 1/4" from the edges of the quilt. This keeps the layers from shifting and the edges from stretching while you are applying the binding. A single, straight-of-grain binding cut at 1-1/4" and sewn with a 1/4" seam will finish to 1/4".

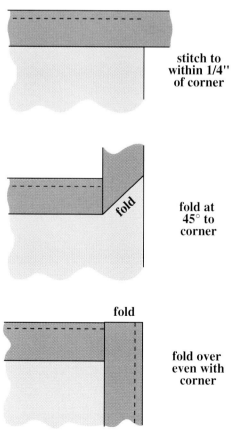

stitch to within 1/4" of corner

fold at 45° to corner

fold over even with corner

All bindings are put on in one continuous strip, mitering at each corner. This is easy to do, and gives a professional finishing touch to your quilt. To make a mitered corner, sew up to 1/4" from the corner; stop and backstitch. Remove your quilt from the machine, pull the binding straight up at right angles from the quilt, and then fold it back down, having the fold even with the edge of the quilt. Begin stitching at the fold. Do each corner the same.

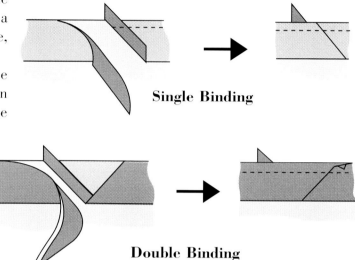

Single Binding

Double Binding

To begin and end the binding easily, start with a 45-degree angle (cut this with your Easy Angle). Press this raw edge under 1/4". Begin with this edge, and when you have gone all the way around the quilt, simply overlap the beginning about 1". Trim off the excess.

⊞ DRAFTING YOUR OWN DESIGNS

Perhaps you have a favorite quilt you would like to miniaturize, a big quilt design that you would like to explore in miniature first, or an interesting block you would like to experiment with in many different versions. All are excellent reasons for drafting your own designs in miniature. The only supplies you need are 4-squares-to-the-inch graph paper, a pencil, eraser, and small ruler.

Begin by determining whether your quilt is a 4-patch, 9-patch or another mathematical division. Does it divide evenly into 4 sections or 6 or 9?

Look carefully at the block and find the smallest unit. Ask yourself just how small you want the finished unit to be. It is important to start with the smallest unit, and scale the other units from that size. Generally, for my smallest miniatures, I base everything on a 1" strip, with the squares or triangle squares finishing to 1/2". An even-sized strip and even-sized finished units are the easiest to work with.

Using the EZ tools makes scaling down a quilt block easy. Look at this example:

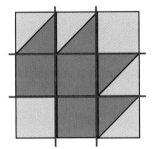

12" block Each unit finishes to 4". Cut 4-1/2" strips.

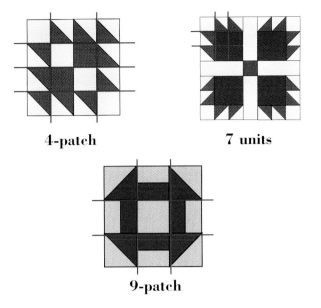

4-patch　　　　　**7 units**

9-patch

9" block Each unit finishes to 3". Cut 3-1/2" strips.

6" block Each unit finishes to 2". Cut 2-1/2" strips.

3" block Each unit finishes to 1". Cut 1-1/2" strips.

1-1/2" block Each unit finishes to 1/2". Cut 1" strips.

Each time, cut the strips 1/2" larger than the finished size of the units to allow for seams. What could be simpler?

❖ TRIANGLE TABLES

Use these triangle tables to determine the number of triangles you can cut from a 42" strip of fabric. Then you can figure out the number of strips to cut (and the fabric you need) if you are designing your own project, or changing the size of one of the projects

NOTE: If the fabric width is more or less than 42", the number of triangles that each strip yields may vary slightly.

Easy Angle

Finished Size	Strip Width	Number
1/2"	1"	50
3/4"	1-1/4"	42
1"	1-1/2"	38
1-1/4"	1-3/4"	32
1-1/2"	2"	30
1-3/4"	2-1/4"	28
2"	2-1/2"	26
2-1/4"	2-3/4"	24
2-1/2"	3"	22
2-3/4"	3-1/4"	20
3"	3-1/2"	20
3-1/4"	3-3/4"	18
3-1/2"	4"	18
3-3/4"	4-1/4"	16
4"	4-1/2"	16
4-1/4"	4-3/4"	14
4-1/2"	5"	14
4-3/4"	5-1/4"	14
5"	5-1/2"	12
5-1/4"	5-3/4"	12
5-1/2"	6"	12
5-3/4"	6-1/4"	12
6"	6-1/2"	12

Companion Angle

Finished Size	Strip Width	Number
1"	1"	34
1-1/2"	1-1/4"	27
2"	1-1/2"	23
2-1/2"	1-3/4"	20
3"	2"	17
3-1/2"	2-1/4"	16
4"	2-1/2"	13
4-1/2"	2-3/4"	13
5"	3"	12
5-1/2"	3-1/4"	10
6"	3-1/2"	9
6-1/2"	3-3/4"	9
7"	4"	8
7-1/2"	4-1/4"	7
8"	4-1/2"	7
8-1/2"	4-3/4"	7
9"	5"	7
9-1/2"	5-1/4"	5
10"	5-1/2"	5

Tri-Recs Triangle Tables

Finished Size	Strip Width	# of Tri Triangles	# of Recs Triangles
1"	1-1/2"	38	52
1-1/2"	2"	31	44
2"	2-1/2"	25	40
2-1/2"	3"	21	34
3"	3-1/2"	19	32
3-1/2"	4"	17	28
4"	4-1/2"	15	24
4-1/2"	5"	13	24
5"	5-1/2"	12	22
5-1/2"	6"	11	22
6"	6-1/2"	10	20

❖ THE BASICS OF APPLIQUÉ

Appliqué is the process by which you apply a shape that is cut from fabric onto a background. This may be done by hand or by machine. Several methods of hand appliqué will be explained here.

There are many different methods of appliqué, and I urge you to experiment until you find the technique that suits you best. Appliqué is wonderful because it allows you to create soft, curved, and naturalistic shapes that just aren't possible with piecing.

Needleturn appliqué:

This is the oldest, and certainly the simplest, way of appliquéing. A template, the exact finished size, is made first, either from stiff paper or template plastic. This shape is then traced around on the right side of your fabric. Cut out the shape by eye, adding between 1/8" to 1/4" seam allowance. Clip any outside curves so when the edges are turned, it will lie flat. This shape is then applied to the background of the block with tiny overcast, blind, or hem stitches. Generally, it is a good idea to match the thread to the color of the shape you are appliquéing. (Silk thread is wonderful, as it "melts" into the fabric. You only need an off-white, a medium tan, and a dark taupe to appliqué any color.) Turn under the seam allowance, including the pencil line, with your needle as you sew the shape.

A variation on the needleturn method involves cutting the template from Mylar plastic (this is plastic that does not melt with the heat of an iron). Cut out your shape as before, only this time mark the fabric on the back. Use the plastic template as a guide to fold the seam allowances over. Press the seam allowances down with your iron, with the plastic template still in place. This results in a nice turned-under edge to appliqué. Remove the template before stitching.

Freezer paper appliqué:

This method is similar to the other methods, except that the finished size template is cut from freezer paper. Iron the template, waxy side down, to the back of your fabric. Cut out the shape, adding 1/8" to 1/4" seam allowance by eye. Clip any outside curves so the shape will lie flat when stitched down. You will find that freezer paper stabilizes the fabric, making it easier to cut. With your thumbnail or the tip of your iron, you can crease the seam allowance under, using the freezer paper template as a guide. Appliqué with the freezer paper in place, or remove the freezer paper before you appliqué. If you leave the freezer paper on the shape, you will have to remove it shortly before you finish appliquéing, or slit the background behind the appliqué and pull out the freezer paper.

Fusible appliqué:

For this method, make a template out of stiff paper or plastic the finished size of your shape, or trace the shape directly from your pattern onto the paper side of the fusible webbing. (Whichever brand of fusible webbing you choose, be sure to use a lightweight kind with paper on one side and bonding material on both sides.) Then roughly cut out the shape on the fusible webbing, iron that shape to the wrong side of the fabric, and carefully cut it out to the exact finished size. Peel off the paper and iron the shape in place on your block. (NOTE: Be sure to read and follow the package directions for using the fusible webbing.)

Some people do not care for the stiffness the fusible webbing adds to a shape. To avoid some of that stiffness, you can cut the centers out of the shapes. For example, to appliqué an apple on a quilt, trace the apple shape onto the fusible webbing paper. Roughly cut out that apple shape. Carefully cut 1/4" inside the apple drawn on the fusible webbing, discarding the center. Apply the fusible webbing shape to the back of your fabric. Cut out the apple shape on the pencil line. You will finish with an apple that has only the fusible webbing 1/4" from the edge of the shape all around, leaving the center "soft." This method works very nicely for machine appliqué, or when you are adding a buttonhole stitch to the outside edge of each patch.

❖ NARROW BIAS STEMS

There are several methods for making narrow stems:

Method A: Cut a **bias** strip three times as wide as you want the finished stem. For example, to make a finished stem of 1/4", cut a 3/4" bias strip. Mark a line on your background fabric where you want the stem to be placed. Lay the bias strip in place over this line. Sew (by hand or machine) on this line 1/4" from the edge of the bias strip. Turn under 1/4" and stitch down the other side of the stem by hand.

Method B: Using Bias Press Bars, or electrical ties purchased in an automotive supply store (which are made to withstand high heat), you can make long strips of bias tubing easily and rapidly. For a 1/4" finished stem, cut 1" wide bias strips. Fold wrong sides together and stitch a careful 1/4" seam. Trim the seam allowance to 1/8". Insert the pressing bar into the tube, and turn the tube so the seam is on a flat side of the pressing bar. (You want the seam to be on the underside of the stem.) Using a hot dry iron, press the seam flat. (You may wish to dampen with water or spray starch.) Remove the **hot** press bar and stitch the bias stem into place with appliqué stitches.

TOOL TUTORIAL

✦ TRI-RECS™ TOOLS

To cut Tri triangles, lay the tool on the strip with the top flat edge at the top of the strip, and a line on the tool aligned with the bottom of the strip. Cut on both sides of the triangle. The patterns will tell you what size strip to cut—always 1/2" larger than the finished size.

To cut Recs triangles, cut the same size strip as for the large triangles. Leave the strip folded and you will automatically cut *pairs* of Recs triangles. Align the tool with the flat top edge at the top of the strip, and a line on the tool aligned with the bottom of the strip. Cut on the angled edge, then swing around and nip off the "magic angle" at the top. This needs to be cut accurately, as it is your alignment guide when sewing the pieces together.

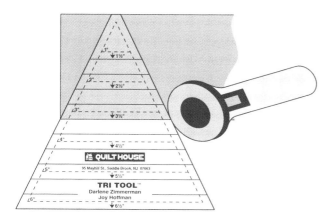

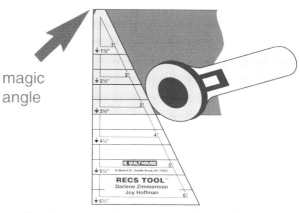

For the second cut, rotate the tool so it is pointing down. Align as before and cut.

For the second cut, rotate the tool so it is pointing down. Align as before and cut, then swing back and trim off the "magic angle."

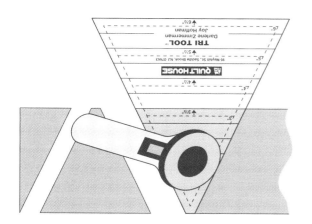

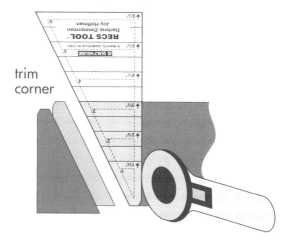

Together the two tools cut the shapes for making a triangle within a square. Lay out the pieces as shown to form a square.

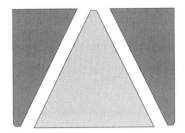

Fit the Recs triangle into the corner of the large triangle. Note how the "magic angle" will fit right into the corner as shown. Yes, the pieces look odd at this point, but they will be right when sewn!

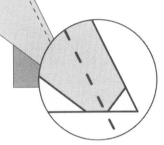

Piecing Rectangles

Place two Recs triangles right sides together, fitting the "magic angle" into the corner as shown. Stitch and press toward the darker fabric.

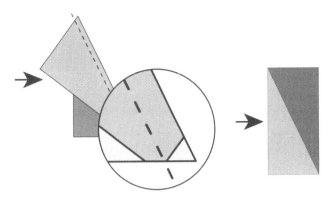

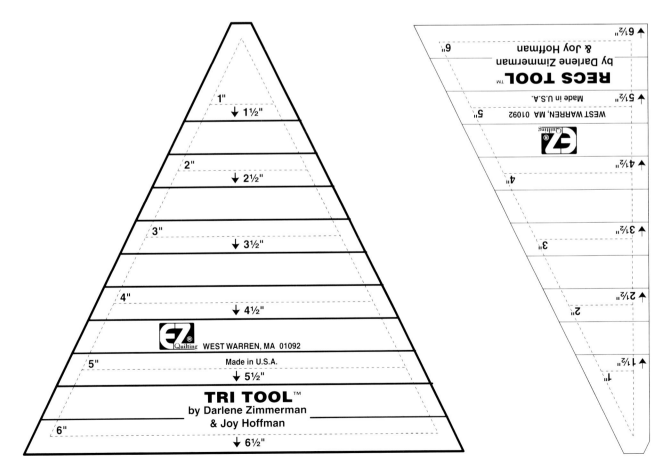

❖ EASY ANGLE™

This tool comes in two different sizes, 4-1/2" and 6-1/2". You may use either one for the projects in this book. Easy Angle allows you to cut triangle squares from the same size strip as for squares. You only need to add a 1/2" seam allowance when using Easy Angle (instead of that nasty 7/8" you add when cutting squares, then cutting on the diagonal).

To use the tool most efficiently, layer the fabric strips you are using for your triangle squares right sides together, then cut with Easy Angle. They will then be ready to chain-sew.

Before making the first cut, trim off the selvages. Then align the top flat edge of the tool at the top of the strip, matching a line on the tool with the bottom edge of the strip. Cut on the diagonal edge.

To make the second cut, rotate the tool so the flat edge is aligned at the bottom of the strip, and a line on the tool is aligned with the top of the strip. Cut again.

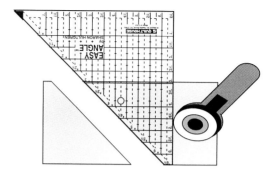

Continue in this manner down the strip. Chain-sew the triangles on the longest edge. Press toward the darkest fabric and trim dog-ears.

NOTE: If you choose not to use Easy Angle in the projects, you will need to add 7/8" to all the finished sizes of the units. Then cut a strip that width. For example, instead of cutting a 1" strip to yield 1/2" triangle squares, cut a 1-3/8" strip instead. Then cut squares, and cut the squares once on the diagonal.

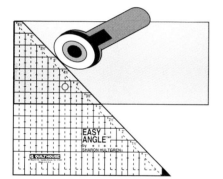

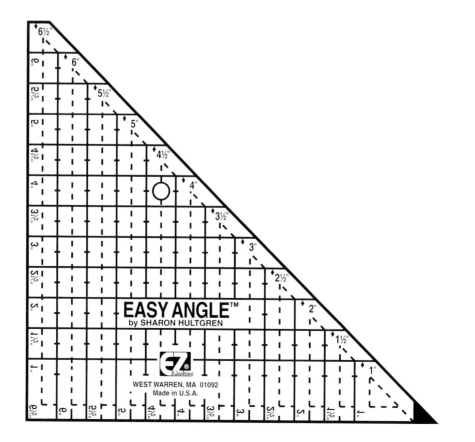

COMPANION ANGLE™

Companion Angle allows you to cut quarter-square triangles—or triangles with the longest edge on the straight of grain. A common use for this type of triangle is the "goose" in flying geese.

To cut with Companion Angle, align the top flat point of the tool with the top edge of the strip. A line on the tool should align with the bottom of the strip. Cut on both sides of the tool.

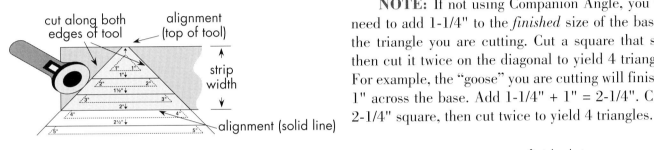

cut along both edges of tool
alignment (top of tool)
strip width
alignment (solid line)

For the next cut, rotate the tool so the point of the tool is at the bottom of the strip, and a line on the tool

is aligned with the bottom of the strip. Cut again.

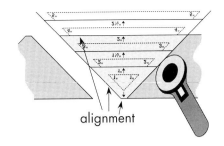

alignment

Continue in this manner down the strip of fabric.

NOTE: If not using Companion Angle, you will need to add 1-1/4" to the *finished* size of the base of the triangle you are cutting. Cut a square that size, then cut it twice on the diagonal to yield 4 triangles. For example, the "goose" you are cutting will finish to 1" across the base. Add 1-1/4" + 1" = 2-1/4". Cut a 2-1/4" square, then cut twice to yield 4 triangles.

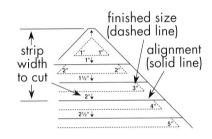

finished size (dashed line)
alignment (solid line)
strip width to cut

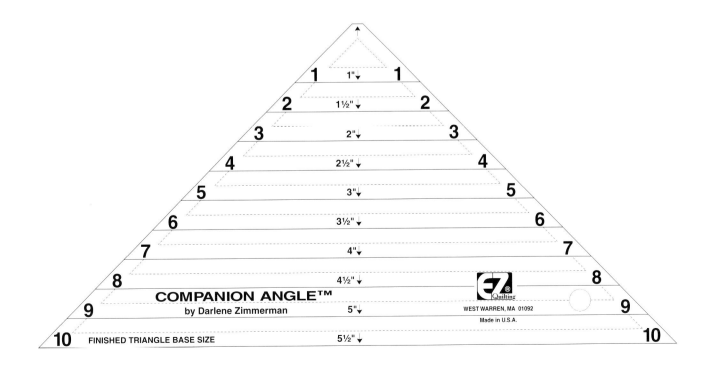

COMPANION ANGLE™
by Darlene Zimmerman
FINISHED TRIANGLE BASE SIZE

1 — 1" — 1
2 — 1½" — 2
3 — 2" — 3
4 — 2½" — 4
5 — 3" — 5
6 — 3½" — 6
7 — 4" — 7
8 — 4½" — 8
9 — 5" — 9
10 — 5½" — 10

EZ Quilting
WEST WARREN, MA 01092
Made in U.S.A.

✳ EASY EIGHT™

Easy Eight allows you to cut diamonds of various sizes without a template. Use the tool as a ruler to cut the strip for the size diamond you have chosen.

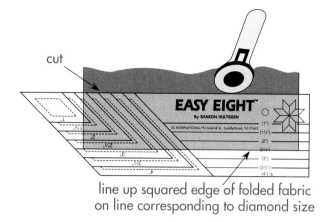

line up squared edge of folded fabric on line corresponding to diamond size

Slide the tool on the end of the strip, trimming off the first angle.

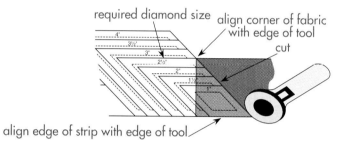

required diamond size — align corner of fabric with edge of tool — cut

align edge of strip with edge of tool

Slide the tool further along the strip until the entire diamond is filled up. Cut again.

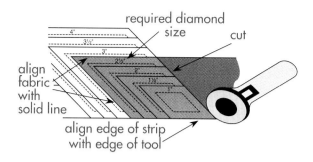

required diamond size — cut

align fabric with solid line

align edge of strip with edge of tool

Continue in this manner down the strip.

All these tools can be found at your local quilt, craft or fabric store. If you cannot find them locally, you may call 1-800-660-0415 to order from EZ Quilting by Wrights.

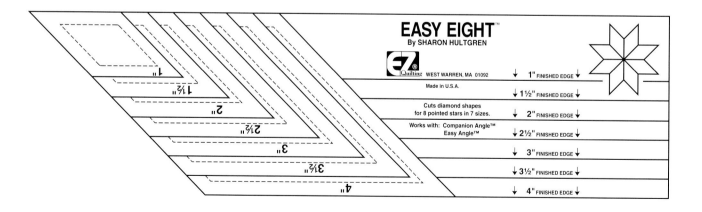

EASY EIGHT™
By SHARON HULTGREN

EZ Quilting WEST WARREN, MA 01092
Made in U.S.A.

Cuts diamond shapes for 8 pointed stars in 7 sizes.

Works with: Companion Angle™ Easy Angle™

↓ 1" FINISHED EDGE ↓
↓ 1½" FINISHED EDGE ↓
↓ 2" FINISHED EDGE ↓
↓ 2½" FINISHED EDGE ↓
↓ 3" FINISHED EDGE ↓
↓ 3½" FINISHED EDGE ↓
↓ 4" FINISHED EDGE ↓

Winter Quilts

BALTIMORE WEDDING ALBUM

Quilt 1

(12-1/2" square, 3-1/2" block)

This is a tiny (fused only) version of a Baltimore Album quilt with embellishments.

Fabric Requirements
Background: 1/4 yard
Green print: 1/4 yard
Scraps of red and gold

Additional Supplies
1 yard fusible webbing
(with paper on one side)
Template plastic
Optional embellishments
such as tiny beads or buttons
Green embroidery floss

Directions

Cut nine 4" blocks from background fabric. Fold and crease (or mark) the center of each block horizontally and vertically. Sew the blocks together in rows of three. Join the rows to make the quilt top. Cut two 1-1/2" green print strips for the border. Sew the borders to the quilt. The fusing is done after the piecing, as the less you handle the quilt after you have done the fusing, the better.

Trace the required number of leaves, hearts, circles and flowers on the paper side of the fusible webbing. Trace directly from the templates given in this book or cut templates from template plastic. When tracing the shapes, group all the pieces to be cut from green together on your paper. Do the same for the pieces to be cut from red and gold. Fuse the groupings of pieces onto the wrong side of the fabrics you are using. Now you can cut the leaves, hearts, etc.

individually.

(***HINT***: To help prevent the small pieces from fraying, spray-starch the fabrics on the right side to give them more body and to add a finish on the fabric.)

(***HINT:*** Do you have difficulty pulling the paper off the back of the small pieces? To make this much easier, loosen a portion of each roughly cut shape before you cut out the individual pieces.)

Using the block drawings and the horizontal and vertical lines as a guide, position the shapes on each of the blocks and fuse. (***TIP:*** You will be able to pull them up and reposition them if you touch them lightly with the iron, and pull them up while they are still warm.) Remember to work in layers, fusing the bottom layer of the appliqué first, and adding additional layers one at a time. Don't hesitate to experiment with designing your own blocks with the shapes given here.

Embellishment

Complete the center block with outline-stitch embroidered stems. Use a ruler to mark the stem lines lightly. Embroider with two strands of floss. Embroidered stems may also be added in some of the other blocks. Beads can be used in the center of the flowers, or just as berries in the leaf wreath, and sewn on either before or after the quilting is completed.

Quilting Suggestions

If you were to quilt the background in this quilt as heavily as in the large Baltimore Album, the appliqué would "float" and the edges would pull loose, especially with all the handling dur-

12-1/2" square

ing the quilting process. Use only a minimal amount of quilting—just machine stitching in the ditch created by the seams, sewing with matching thread. This is all that is necessary to enhance the blocks.

Binding

Before binding, hand-baste a scant 1/4" from the edge of the quilt.

Cut two 1-1/4" green strips. Join the binding strips with diagonal seams pressed open and trimmed to 1/4". Sew the binding strips to the quilt with a 1/4" seam. (See page 12 for instructions on binding and mitered corners.) Trim the excess backing and batting even with the quilt top. Turn binding under 1/4", turn to the back side, covering the stitching line. Sew down by hand with matching thread.

BALTIMORE WEDDING ALBUM
Quilt 2
(28" square, 7" block)

Fabric Requirements

Background Fabric: 1/2 yard beige solid, print, small plaid or check

Red: Variety of coordinating scraps

Green: 2/3 yard for border and binding, and a variety of scraps for leaves

Black: 1/8 yard (used for inside border only)

Additional Supplies

2 yards fusible webbing with paper on one side

Old buttons

Black embroidery floss or #8 pearl cotton (if button-hole stitching by hand)

28" square

Appliquéing the blocks

Cut nine blocks 7-1/2" square from background fabric. Crease the block horizontally, vertically, and diagonally. Notice only Block 1 and 2 from **Baltimore Wedding Album, Quilt 3** have been used in this quilt. Trace 36 small flowers and 72 large leaves onto the paper side of the fusible web, leaving at least 1/4" between each shape. Cut the shapes out roughly, then iron to the back of the red and green fabrics. Cut out the shapes on the marked line, then peel off the paper. Fuse a 5" x 4" rectangle of fusible web to the back side of a green print. Rotary cut 10 stems measuring 1/4" x 4".

Fuse the stems, leaves, and flowers into position on the blocks, using the crease marks for guidance. When all the blocks are completed, buttonhole stitch around all the leaves and flowers by machine or by hand. Use an outline stitch on both sides of the stems instead of buttonhole stitching.

When the blocks are finished, join them block to block.

Borders

Cut four 1" strips of black fabric for the inside border. Cut four 3-1/2" strips of green fabric for the outside borders. Sew the black and green strips together. Press toward the green border. Sew the borders to the quilt, mitering the corners. (See pg. 11 for instruction on mitering corners.)

Quilting suggestions

Quilt in the ditch around each of the motifs by hand or by machine. To fill in the background behind the motifs, cross-hatching may be used, or, simpler and just as effective, diagonal lines 1/2" apart. Also, stitch in the ditch around the inside and outside borders. A pretty border design enhances the wide border.

Embellishment

A variety of old brown and tan buttons were used for the center of the flowers after the quilting was finished. The buttons were attached with black thread.

Binding

Before binding, hand-baste a scant 1/4" from the edge of the quilt.

Cut four 1-1/4" strips of green fabric. Join the binding strips with diagonal seams pressed open and trimmed to 1/4". Sew the binding strips to the quilt with a 1/4" seam. (See page 12 for instructions on binding and mitered corners.) Trim the excess backing and batting even with the quilt top. Turn binding under 1/4", turn to the back side, covering the stitching line. Sew down by hand with matching thread.

BALTIMORE WEDDING ALBUM

Quilt 3

(31" square, 7" block)

At the time this quilt was made, I was documenting a number of antique appliqué quilts from the 1850-1900s era. Naturally I coveted them, but not being able to afford one of these beautiful quilts, I decided to make my own in miniature. Using just a few simple shapes and arranging them in various ways, I was able to create nine different blocks. Don't be afraid to play with these shapes to design your own blocks, or to cut different flowers or leaves and arrange them to suit yourself. If you don't enjoy the hand appliqué, try one of the other versions of this quilt which use fusible appliqué.

Fabric Requirements
Background: 1 yard
Green Print: 1-1/2 yards
Red Print: 1/4 yard
Gold Print: Scraps or 1/8 yard
Optional: Small buttons or beads for "berries" on the leaf wreath block

Directions

If you are unfamiliar with hand appliqué, read through the section at the beginning of the book on this topic. Choose the appliqué method you prefer, and then cut the required number of leaves, hearts, flowers and circles from fabrics. Cut 9 squares of background fabric measuring 7-1/2". You also need to make some bias stems using whichever method you prefer (refer to pgs. 15-16 in the instructions at the beginning of the book).

Use the full-size drawings to mark the placement of the shapes on your background squares. (**HINT:** Use the blue washout marker, then when the appliqué work is finished, you can remove the marks by soaking in cold water.) Or you can simply crease the center of the block horizontally, vertically, and

31" square

diagonally, and use these crease marks as placement guides. Cut out the required number of shapes for each block, adding seam allowances. Pin or baste the shapes into position, then appliqué them down.

When all the blocks are completed, arrange them in a pleasing and balanced manner. Cut three 1-1/2" strips of green fabric. From these strips cut 12 sashing strips 1-1/2" x 7-1/2". Also cut one 1-1/2" strip of red fabric. Cut into eight corner squares. Join the blocks with sashing strips and corner squares.

Borders

Cut four green strips 1-1/2" wide. Measure and cut 4 borders the *width* of the quilt. Sew to the top and bottom of the quilt. Press the seam toward the border.

Sew the red corner stones to the ends of both remaining border strips. Press the seams toward the green strips. Sew to the sides of the quilt. Press the seams toward the green border.

Cut four 4" outside border strips of background fabric, and four 1-1/4" wide final borders of green fabric. Sew the background and green border strips together, the length of the fabric. Sew the borders to the quilt, mitering the corners so they do not interfere with the appliqué in the wide border. (See pg. 11 for instruction on mitering corners.)

Cut a paper border the same size as one of the background fabric quilt borders to plan the borders on paper first. Plan the placement of the vine on the border so it undulates gracefully and evenly on each side. After the vine is planned, add the leaves and flowers along the vine. When satisfied with the arrangement, use the paper pattern to mark the appliqué placement on the quilt borders.

Appliqué the vine first, and then the leaves and flowers, using flowers in the corners to cover the ends of the vines.

Quilting suggestions

On many fine antique appliqué quilts, you will see diagonal stitching lines in the background. This is a lovely way to fill the background behind the appliqué without detracting from the motifs. The quilt shown has lines stitched 3/8" apart on the diagonal in each of the blocks, and I also stitched in the ditch around each of the motifs to make them stand out. "Echo" quilting was done in the border around the vine and each of the motifs. To do this, stitch one line of quilting close to each of the motifs, connecting them. Continue stitching lines 1/4" apart by eye until the entire area is filled. Yes, there is quite a bit of quilting on this quilt, but it was very enjoyable, especially since each block is different. The results were well worth the effort.

Binding

Before binding, hand-baste a scant 1/4" from the edge of the quilt.

Cut four 1-1/4" strips of green fabric. Join the binding strips with diagonal seams pressed open and trimmed to 1/4". Sew the binding strips to the quilt with a 1/4" seam. (See page 12 for instructions on binding and mitered corners.) Trim the excess backing and batting even with the quilt top. Turn binding under 1/4", turn to the back side, covering the stitching line. Sew down by hand with matching thread.

MINIATURE BEAR'S PAW

(11-3/4" square, 3-1/2" block)

with The Bear Went Over the Mountain optional border

Tool Requirements	**Fabric Requirements**
Easy Angle	Background: 1/4 yard
Companion Angle	Print for border: 1/4 yard
(for optional border)	Red print: 1/4 yard
	Black: 1/4 yard

11-3/4" Square

40

There is an interesting story told about the origins of the Bear's Paw block. This story comes from the pages of a young man's diary during the pioneer days in Ohio.

A young man went out from Connecticut in 1836 and settled in Ohio. He was twenty-four years old. A few farms had been cleared, but the majority of the land still stood in virgin forest. The job of this young pioneer was to turn, with his own hands, 160 acres of densely wooded country into open fields and pastures. It was hard work, but he found satisfaction in it. There was only one problem in his life, and her name was Mary Ann.

Later pictures show Mary Ann must have been as pretty as paint, a little bit of a girl, as slender and delicate as the young pioneer was husky and tall. It was inevitable that he should adore her. But he was not the only young lad who had come West to seek his fortune. She had the pick of two counties and for a long while she kept him guessing. Finally, having "yanked" enough stumps to plant a few acres to crop, her wood-chopping lover pronounced an ultimatum. After work, in one week's time, he would come calling once more for her answer, when she must take him or leave him. And that was that.

In the late afternoon of the appointed day, he started out on his three-mile hike through the forest, carrying his gun, and dreaming of the "yes" he hoped for at the end of his journey. He must have been dreaming, for otherwise, woodsman as he was, he wouldn't have left his gun against a tree when he stopped to pick some wild flowers for his lady. But he did, and along came a mother bear, ferocious and hungry from cubbing. He could not reach his gun. Realizing the bear was heavy with milk and could not climb; he "shinnied" up a tree—and there he sat from five o'clock that evening until almost noon the next day, when Mrs. Bear finally ambled off.

Meanwhile, Mary Ann was beside herself, and had all night to tearfully conclude that she had flirted once too often. When, many hours late, the disheveled young man appeared at her door with this bear story up his sleeve, she accepted both him and his yarn, and they lived happily ever after. When they were married, the neighbors presented them with a "Bear's Paw" quilt.

Cutting directions

CUT	TO YIELD
Background Fabric	
4 - 1" strips	16 squares
	64 Easy Angle triangles*
	16 sashings 1" x 2"
Print Fabric	
1 - 1-1/2" strip	16 squares
1 - 1-3/4" strip	Outside border
Red Fabric	
2 - 1" strips	64 Easy Angle triangles*
	1 square (for center of sashing)
Black Fabric	
2 - 1" strips	4 squares
	Sashing strips
	Inside border
2 - 1-1/4" strips	Binding

*Layer background and red fabrics right sides together and cut with Easy Angle. They will then be ready to chain-sew.
NOTE: If not using Easy Angle, cut 1-3/8" squares. Cut once on the diagonal.

Assembling the quilt

Assemble all the triangle squares. Press toward the darkest fabric. Trim dog-ears. Lay out one "paw." Notice how both sets of triangles point to the corner.

Assemble 16 pairs of triangles facing one direction, and 16 pairs facing the other direction. (**NOTE:** All the paws are the same, only turned.)

Make 16   Make 16

Add the background square to your first set of triangle pairs, pressing the seam to the small square.

Make 16

Add the other triangle set to the large square, pressing the seam toward the large square.

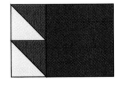

Make 16

Sew the units together to complete one paw.

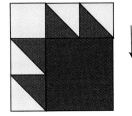

Make 16

41

Lay out one block, turning the paws so they face the right direction. Add the background sashing strips and the black center square. Sew the sashings between the paws, pressing the seams toward the sashing. Assemble all four blocks in this manner.

Make 4

When the blocks are assembled, add the black sashing strips between the blocks. Measure and cut two narrow black borders the *width* of the quilt. Sew to the top and bottom of the quilt. Press the seams toward the black border.

Measure and cut two borders the *length* of the quilt. Sew to the sides of the quilt and press the seams toward the border.

Add the print outside borders in the same manner.

Quilting suggestions

By hand or by machine, quilt in the ditch around each of the paws, and between the inside and outside borders. If additional quilting is desired, you could also quilt a design in the borders.

Binding

Before binding, hand-baste a scant 1/4" from the edge of the quilt.

Join the binding strips with diagonal seams pressed open and trimmed to 1/4". Sew the binding strips to the quilt with a 1/4" seam. (See page 12 for instructions on binding and mitered corners.) Trim the excess backing and batting even with the quilt top. Turn binding under 1/4", turn to the back side, covering the stitching line. Sew down by hand with matching thread.

Miniature Bear's Paw with Bear Went Over the Mountain border 12" Square

Directions for The Bear Went Over the Mountain border

CUT	TO YIELD
Background Fabric	
3 - 1" strips	20 squares
	80 Easy Angle triangles*
Print Fabric for Border	
1 - 1" strip	Second border
1 - 1-1/8" strip	20 Companion Angle triangles (for paws)
2 - 1-1/2" strips	24 Companion Angle setting triangles
Red Fabric	
2 - 1" strips	96 Easy Angle triangles* of which 16 will be orphans

*Layer background and accent fabrics right sides together and cut with Easy Angle. They are then ready to chain sew.

NOTE: If not using Easy Angle, cut 1-3/8" squares. Cut once on the diagonal. If not using Companion Angle, cut 3" squares and 3-1/4" squares respectively. Cut twice on the diagonal.

Border assembly

Instead of the 1-3/4" print border, add a 1" print border, mitering the corners. (See pg. 11 for instruction on mitering corners.)

Assemble 20 paws according to previous directions. They will look somewhat different, because you are adding them to the *smaller* of the two sizes of Companion Angle triangles you have cut from the print.

Make 20

Add small red triangles (the "orphans") to the right side of 16 of the paws, and the larger print triangles to the left side of every paw.

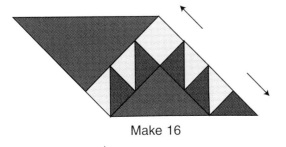
Make 16

Add the remaining four large print triangles to the right side of the four paws without the small red triangles. These will become the right hand corners of each border.

Make 4

Assemble four mitered borders with five paws in each border. Add the borders to the quilt. (**TIP:** The inside borders of print can be adjusted—wider or narrower—to accommodate the pieced borders. When you have a large number of seams in a piece, tiny discrepancies can throw off the final measurement.)

Quilting suggestions

By hand or by machine, quilt in the ditch between the inside borders, and between the print border and the pieced border. Quilt in the ditch around the outside of each of the paws.

Binding

Before binding, hand-baste a scant 1/4" from the edge of the quilt.

Join the binding strips with diagonal seams pressed open and trimmed to 1/4". Sew the binding strips to the quilt with a 1/4" seam. (See page 12 for instructions on binding and mitered corners.) Trim the excess backing and batting even with the quilt top. Turn binding under 1/4", turn to the back side, covering the stitching line. Sew down by hand with matching thread.

(**NOTE:** Congratulations on finishing this project. Now that you've finished, I can tell you this small quilt contains a total of 425 pieces! Aren't you glad you didn't know that earlier?)

20-1/2" Square

LARGE BEAR'S PAW

(20-1/2" square, 7" block)

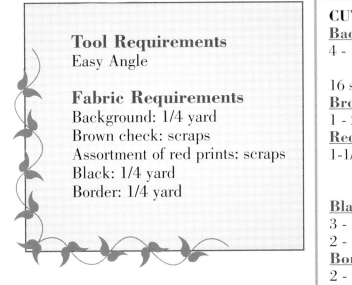

Tool Requirements
Easy Angle

Fabric Requirements
Background: 1/4 yard
Brown check: scraps
Assortment of red prints: scraps
Black: 1/4 yard
Border: 1/4 yard

CUT	TO YIELD
Background Fabric	
4 - 1-1/2" strips	16 squares
	64 Easy Angle triangles*
16 sashing strips - 1-1/2" x 3-1/2"	
Brown Check	
1 - 2-1/2" strip	16 squares
Red Prints	
1-1/2" strips	64 Easy Angle triangles*
	4 squares (block centers)
	1 - 1" square
Black	
3 - 1" strips	Sashing and inside border
2 - 1-1/4" strips	Binding
Border	
2 - 3" strips	Outside border

*Layer background and red print strips right sides together and cut with Easy Angle. They will then be ready to chain-sew.

NOTE: If not using Easy Angle, cut 1-7/8" squares. Cut once on the diagonal.

Quilt assembly
Follow directions for assembly as given in the miniature pattern.

Quilting suggestions
You may wish to quilt a design in each of the large squares in the "paws" that make up a block. Or, quilt diagonal parallel lines following the diagonal lines of the triangles in each paw, and one line from corner to corner. Quilt in the ditch around each block and around the inside border. Quilt a design in the border.

Binding
Before binding, hand-baste a scant 1/4" from the edge of the quilt.

Join the binding strips with diagonal seams pressed open and trimmed to 1/4". Sew the binding strips to the quilt with a 1/4" seam. (See page 12 for instructions on binding and mitered corners.) Trim the excess backing and batting even with the quilt top. Turn binding under 1/4", turn to the back side, covering the stitching line. Sew down by hand with matching thread.

CHRISTMAS TULIPS

(18" square, 3-1/2" block)

Tool Requirements	Fabric Requirements
Tri-Recs	Red: 1/4 yard
Companion Angle	Pink: 1/8 yard
Easy Angle	White tone-on-tone: 1 yard
	Dark green print: 1/4 yard

18" Square

Cutting directions

CUT	TO YIELD	CUT	TO YIELD
Red Fabric		**Green Fabric**	
2 - 1-1/2" strips	48 pairs of Recs triangles	2 - 1" strips	16 sashes 1"x4"
2 - 1" strips	60 - 1" squares		5 squares
Pink Fabric		2 - 1" strips	Inside border
2 - 1" strips		2 - 1-1/4" strips	Binding
White Fabric			
2 - 1-1/2" strips	48 pairs of Recs triangles		
2 - 1" strips			
2 - 1-1/2" strips	48 - 1"x1-1/2" rectangles		
1 - 2" strip	20 - 1"x2" sashes between tulips		
3 - 1-3/4" strips	48 Companion Angles triangles (for border)		
1 - 2" strip	8 Easy Angle triangles (for ends of borders)		
1 - 3-1/2" strip	4 Companion Angles triangles		
1 - 4" strip	4 Easy Angle triangles		
1 - 1-1/2" strip	4 - 1-1/2"x2" rectangles (for corner tulips)		
	4 - 1-1/2"x3" rectangles (for corner tulips)		

NOTE: If not using Easy Angle, cut four 2-3/8" squares (for borders) and two 4-3/8" squares for corner squares. Cut once on the diagonal. If not using Companion Angle, cut twelve 3-3/4" squares (for borders) and one 7-1/4" square for setting triangles. Cut twice on the diagonal. There is no easy way to cut the Recs units without the tool.

Tulip blocks

Right sides together, sew the white Recs triangles to red Recs triangles, using the cut-off tip for alignment. Press toward the colored fabric. Make 96 units.

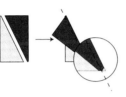

Layer the white and pink 1" strips right sides together. Sew, press and cut into forty-eight 1" x 1-1/2" rectangles.

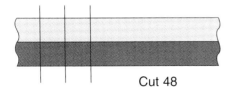

Cut 48

Sew the 1" x 1-1/2" white rectangles to the rectangles you have created with the pink and white strips. Press toward the white rectangle.

Make 48

For each tulip, you will need a pair of Recs units, both a right and left side, a red square for the base of the tulip, and a pink/white center square unit. Assemble as shown, following pressing arrows.

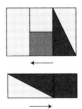

Make 48

Assemble five tulip blocks, using the white sashing and green center squares. Press seams toward the white sashes.

Using the large Companion Angle triangles you have cut for half blocks, and the Easy Angle triangles for the corner blocks, set the tulip blocks on point with green sashings and red stepping stones.

Make 5

Before adding green borders, trim square careful-ly to 12-1/2", leaving 1/4" seam allowance from each of the points.

Inside border

Cut two 1" green border strips the exact *width* of the quilt. Sew to the top and bottom of the quilt and press toward the border.

Cut two 1" green border strips the exact *length* of the quilt. Sew to the sides of the quilt. Press the seams toward the borders.

Tulip border

You will need six tulips set on point for each side of the quilt, not counting the corners. Add Companion

Angle triangles to the upper left and lower right of all the tulips. Press toward the white triangles.

Join six tulips to make one border. Add Easy Angle triangles on both ends. Press. Trim to 1/4" seam allowance at the base of the tulips, and also at the top if needed to make the border 3" wide. Trim both ends evenly so the border meas-ures 3" x 13-1/2". Assemble the remain-ing three borders in the same man-ner.

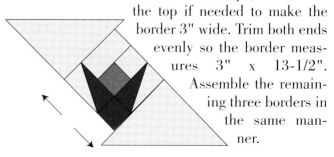

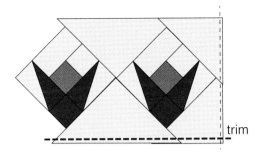

trim

For the corner tulips, add the 1-1/2" x 2" white rectangle to one top edge of the tulip to form a rectangle. Add the 1-1/2" x 3" white rectangle on an adjacent side to form a square.

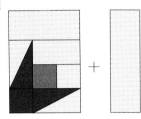

Add two of the pieced borders to opposite sides of the quilt. Press toward the green border.

Add corner blocks to the remaining two borders, then sew those borders to the sides of the quilt. Press the seams toward the green border.

Quilting suggestions

Quilt by hand or machine in the ditch around each of the tulip blocks. Stitch in the ditch on both sides of the sashing and green border. Quilt a pretty design in the large white triangles.

Binding

After the quilting is complete, baste by hand a scant 1/4" from the edge of the quilt.

Join the binding strips with diagonal seams pressed open and trimmed to 1/4". Sew the binding strips to the quilt with a 1/4" seam. (See page 12 for instructions on binding and mitered corners.) Trim the excess backing and batting even with the quilt top. Turn binding under 1/4", turn to the back side, covering the stitching line. Sew down by hand with matching thread.

DIAMOND STARS I

(17-1/2" square, 2-1/4" block)

This little quilt has the look of a Victorian inlaid wood tabletop. The quilt is a result of challenging myself to make the smallest eight-pointed star possible using the sewing machine.

CUT	TO YIELD
Red Print Fabric	
6 - 1" strips	20 diamonds cut with template
	36 sashing strips 1" x 2-3/4"
	Inside borders
Green Print Fabric	
2 - 1" strips	32 diamonds cut with template
	24 squares
Gold Print Fabric	
2 - 1" strips	52 diamonds cut with template
1 - 3-1/2" strip	4 Easy Angle triangles
	(for corners)
1 - 3" strip	8 Companion Angle triangles
	(for half blocks)
Background Fabric	
2 - 1-1/4" strips	52 squares
2 - 1" strips	52 Companion Angle triangles
Border Print	
2 - 2-1/2" strips	Outside borders
2 - 1-1/4" strips	Binding

NOTE: If not using Easy Angle, cut two squares 3-7/8". Cut once on the diagonal for corners. If not using Companion Angle, cut two 6-1/4" squares. Cut twice on the diagonal. For the small background triangles, cut 13 - 2-1/4" squares. Cut twice on the diagonal.

Tool Requirements
Easy Angle
Companion Angle

Fabric Requirements
Red print: 1/4 yard
Green print: 1/8 yard or scraps
Gold print: 1/4 yard
Background: 1/4 yard
Border print: 1/4 yard

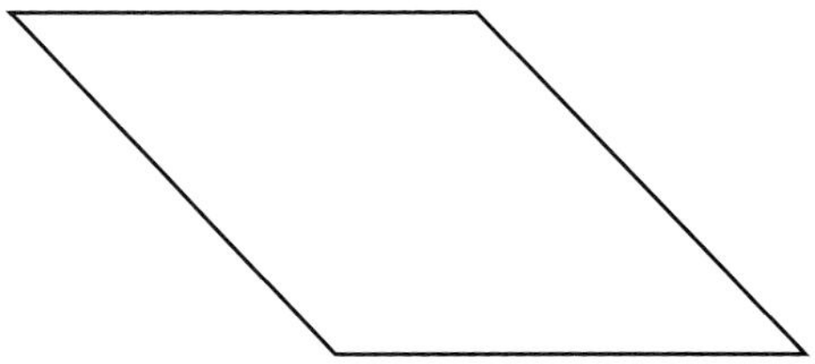

template

17-1/2" Square

If you'd rather use a tool than a template to cut the diamonds, try Diamond Stars II, a slightly larger version.

Star blocks

I suggest you practice the setting in of triangles and squares on a larger scale before you attempt to piece a miniature star. All the techniques are the same, except I finger-pressed the pieces until the star block was completed.

Begin by sewing two diamonds together, a gold diamond to a red or green one. Begin at the *seam*

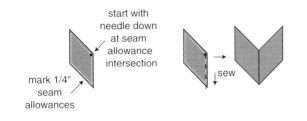

allowance, stitch a few stitches, and then backstitch to lock the seam in place. Stitch to the opposite edge. Press this seam to the left. Join four diamonds.

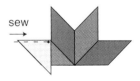

Set in the background triangle and squares as shown. Place a triangle right sides together on top of the diamond, matching raw edges. Stitch toward the center, stopping when you reach the seam intersection, and backstitch.

Turn the half star over and stitch the other edge of the triangle to the next diamond, from the outside edge to the seam intersection. Backstitch. Press the seams toward the diamonds.

Add the square and

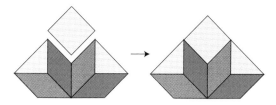

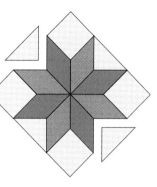

remaining triangle to the half-star. Press all the seams in one direction. Make 10 red-gold half stars, and 16 green-gold half stars.

Join the two half stars, matching the points in the center. Begin stitching at the seam allowance and end at the seam allowance so you can set in the remaining two triangles.

Press the center seam open with the iron and press all the seams flat from the back side of the block. Give each of the blocks a final pressing with steam on the front side, to make them lie as flat as possible, but be careful not to stretch the fabrics. After all the blocks have been pressed, trim (carefully!) to 2-3/4" square.

Lay out the blocks in diagonal rows, placing the five red-gold stars in the center. Add sashes between the blocks.

Join rows of blocks, adding the gold print setting triangles at the ends of the rows. Join the rows, adding sashing strips and corner stones between the rows. Add the corner triangles last. Press all the seams toward the sashing strips. Trim the quilt square, leaving 1/4" seam allowance.

Borders

Measure and cut the red and green borders the width of the quilt, plus two borders and extra inches for insurance. Sew the red and green borders together and press. Sew to the quilt, mitering the corners. See page 11 for instruction on mitering corners.

Quilting suggestions

To make the center of the star lie flat, quilt by hand in the ditch, stitching one line horizontally and one line vertically through each star. (Yes, this can be difficult through all the layers—try stab stitching.) Also quilt in the ditch inside and outside the sashings. Use a simple motif to quilt in the setting triangles on the outside edges of the quilt. Quilt in the ditch on both sides of the inside border and quilt a small design in the outside border if desired.

Binding

Before binding, hand-baste a scant 1/4" from the edge of the quilt.

Join the binding strips with diagonal seams pressed open and trimmed to 1/4". Sew the binding strips to the quilt with a 1/4" seam. (See page 12 for instructions on binding and mitered corners.) Trim the excess backing and batting even with the quilt top. Turn binding under 1/4", turn to the back side, covering the stitching line. Sew down by hand with matching thread.

DIAMOND STARS II

(24-1/2" square, 3-1/2" block)

This is a large variation of Diamond Stars I.

24-1/2" Square

Tool Requirements
Easy Angle
Easy Eight
Companion Angle

Fabric Requirements
Dark purple: 3/8 yard
Print: 3/8 yard
Light purple: 3/8 yard
Background: 1/4 yard
Green: 1/4 yard

CUT	TO YIELD
Dark Purple Fabric	
3 strips with Easy Eight*	52 - 1" diamonds cut with Easy Eight
3 - 1" strips	24 squares
	Inside border
3 - 1-1/4" strips	Binding
Print Fabric	
1 strip with Easy Eight*	20 - 1" diamonds cut with Easy Eight
3 - 3-1/4" strips	Outside border
Light Purple Fabric	
2 strips with Easy Eight*	32 - 1" diamonds cut with Easy Eight
1 - 3-3/4" strip	8 Companion Angle triangles (half blocks)
1 - 4-1/2" strip	4 Easy Angle triangles (corners)
Background Fabric	
2 - 1-1/2" strips	52 squares
2 strips with Easy Eight*	52 Companion Angle triangles
Green Fabric	
1 - 4" strip	36 sashing strips 1"x4"

*Use the 1" cutting line on the Easy Eight tool to cut the strips for the diamonds and the Companion Angle triangles. The strip will NOT measure 1".

NOTE: If not using Easy Eight, cut strips 1-1/4" wide, then cut 45-degree angles every 1-3/4". If not using Easy Angle, cut two 4-7/8" squares. Cut once on the diagonal. If not using Companion Angle, cut two 7-3/4" squares. Cut twice on the diagonal. To cut the small background triangles for the stars, cut 13 - 2-1/2" squares. Cut twice on the diagonal.

Quilt assembly

Follow the directions for assembly, quilting and finishing as given in Diamond Stars I. The blocks are trimmed to 4".

STAR BASKETS

(14" x 18-3/4", 3" block)

Tool Requirements
Easy Angle
Companion Angle
Easy Eight

Fabric Requirements
Red stripe: 1/4 yard
Dark green: 1/4 yard
Background: 1/2 yard

Several years ago, at the AQS show in Paducah, I purchased a red and green quilt top, circa 1875-1900, that featured a simple basket pattern with red star points forming the top of the basket. The red fabric in the star points had a black stripe running through it, and the diamonds were cut and sewn with no regard to the direction of the stripe, which adds interest to an otherwise very simple block. I had to look for a long time to find just the right red and black striped fabric to make my own miniature version of the antique quilt top.

CUT	TO YIELD
Red Fabric	
2 strips at 1" size on Easy Eight*	32 diamonds cut with Easy Eight
2 - 1" strips	Inside border
2 - 1-1/4" strips	Binding
Background Fabric	
1 - 1-1/2" strip	8 squares
1 strip at 1" size on Easy Eight*	16 Companion Angle triangles
1 - 1-1/4" strip	16 rectangles 1-1/4"x2-1/4"
1 - 2" strip	8 Easy Angle triangles
1 - 3-1/2" strip	4 Easy Angle triangles (for corners)
	6 Companion Angle triangles (for half blocks)
2 - 2-1/2" strips	Outside border
Green Fabric	
1 - 1-1/2" strip	8 Companion Angle triangles
1 - 1-1/4" strip	16 Easy Angle triangles

*Use the 1" cutting line on the Easy Eight tool to cut the strips for the diamonds and the Companion Angle triangles.

NOTE: If not using Easy Angle, add 3/8" to the strip size. Cut squares, then cut once on the diagonal.

If not using Companion Angle, cut four 2-1/2" small background squares, two 7-1/4" squares for the half blocks, and two 3-1/4" green squares. Cut twice on the diagonal.

Block assembly

Assemble four red diamonds as shown, beginning at the *seam allowance*, stitching a few stitches, then backstitching to lock that seam in place.

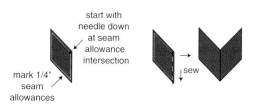

start with needle down at seam allowance intersection

mark 1/4" seam allowances

sew

Set in the background square and triangles as shown. Place the triangle right sides together on top of the red diamond, matching raw edges. Stitch toward the center, stopping when you reach the seam intersection, and backstitch.

sew

56

Turn the half star over and stitch the other edge of the triangle to the next diamond, from the outside edge to the seam intersection. Backstitch. Press the seams toward the diamonds.

Add the bottom large green triangle to form a square.

Add small green triangles to rectangles, making both a right and a left side for the baskets.

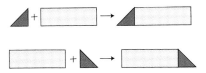

Add to the sides of the baskets. Add the bottom background triangles. The blocks should measure 3-1/2", including seam allowances.

The baskets are set block to block on point, with plain half-blocks and corner blocks.

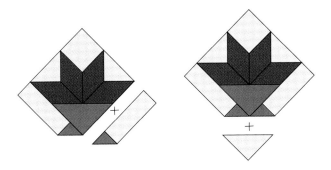

Assemble the quilt in diagonal rows, following the diagram. (**NOTE:** The setting triangles are larger than needed.) Trim square, leaving a 1/4" seam allowance on all four sides.

Sew the red and background borders together, sew them to the quilt, mitering the corners. See page 11 for mitering corners.

Quilting suggestions

Hand or machine quilt in the ditch around each of the diamonds, the baskets, and each of the blocks.

Quilt a pretty motif in each of the half-blocks and corners. Quilt in the ditch on both sides of the red border and quilt a design in the border. Or, if you would rather machine quilt, stipple in the background behind each of the baskets and in the outside border.

Binding

Before binding, hand-baste a scant 1/4" from the edge of the quilt.

Join the binding strips with diagonal seams pressed open and trimmed to 1/4". Sew the binding strips to the quilt with a 1/4" seam. (See page 12 for instructions on binding and mitered corners.) Trim the excess backing and batting even with the quilt top. Turn binding under 1/4", turn to the back side, covering the stitching line. Sew down by hand with matching thread.

TIP: To give the quilt an antique look, tea-dye the entire quilt when it is finished.

Spring Quilts

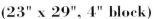

BUTTERFLY GARDEN

(23" x 29", 4" block)

Tool Requirements
Tri-Recs
Companion Angle

Assorted reproduction '30s prints
and solids: scraps or fat quarters
Dark brown or black: scraps

Fabric Requirements
Green print: 3/4 yard.
White: 1/3 yard
Yellow print: 1/8 yard

Additional Supplies
1 yard fusible web
Black embroidery floss (2 strands) or
Pearl Cotton size 8
Blue washout pen

Cutting directions

CUT	TO YIELD	CUT	TO YIELD
Green Print Fabric		**Assorted Print Fabrics**	
2 - 3-1/2" strips	10 Companion Angle triangles	(For *each* flower cut)	
1 - 4" strip	2 - 4" squares,	1 - 2-1/2" strip	4 Tri triangles
	cut once on the diagonal		
3 - 3" strips	Outside border	**Yellow Print Fabric**	
3 - 1-1/4" strips	Binding	3 - 1" strips	Inside border
White Fabric			
1 - 4-1/2" strip	8 - 4-1/2" squares for butterfly blocks		
2 - 2-1/2" strips	40 pairs of Recs triangles,		
	for flower blocks		

NOTE: If not using Companion Angle, cut three 7-1/4" squares. Cut twice on the diagonal. There is no other easy way to cut the Tri-Recs pieces.

Butterfly blocks assembly

Trace both sets of butterfly wings and a butterfly body separately on the paper side of fusible web eight times, leaving space between each shape. Roughly cut out each shape. Following the manufacturer's directions, fuse to the wrong side of the fabrics you have chosen. Cut out on the marked line.

Fuse the butterflies in place on the 4-1/2" white squares, placing the butterflies on the diagonal. Position the lower set of wings under the top set, and the body on top of both sets of wings.

23" x 29"

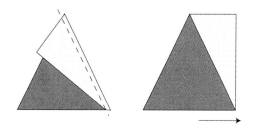

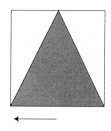

the units you have just pressed. Fit the "magic angle" into the adjacent corner of the large triangle. Press the seam toward the white triangle.

Sew four matching Tri-Recs units together to form a flower block, giving the units a quarter turn each time. Press the seams as directed. Make ten flower blocks.

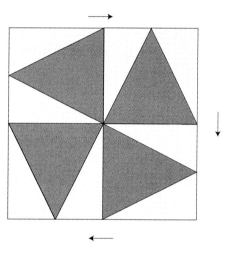

Buttonhole stitch around each of the butterfly's wings and bodies by hand with black floss or pearl cotton, or black thread if using the sewing machine. Trace the antenna markings on the butterfly blocks, and embroider.

Flower block assembly

Assemble four Tri-Recs units for each flower. Sew a white small triangle to the right side of a large print triangle as shown, fitting the "magic angle" into the corner of the large triangle. Press the seam toward the white triangle.

Sew another white triangle to the opposite side of

Quilt assembly

Lay out the flower and butterfly blocks in diagonal rows, filling in the edges with the large green print triangles. Add the smaller triangles in the corners.

Sew the blocks and triangles together in diagonal rows. Press the seams so they alternate. Add the corner triangles last. Press all the seams in one direction.

(***NOTE:*** The side and corner triangles are larger than needed.)

Trim the quilt evenly on all sides. Be sure to leave at least 1/4" or more from the outside corners of the blocks.

Borders

Measure the quilt *width* through the middle, and cut two narrow yellow borders to this length. Sew to the top and bottom of the quilt. Press the seams toward the borders.

Measure the quilt *length* through the middle, and cut two narrow yellow borders to this measurement. Sew to the sides of the quilt and press toward the borders.

Repeat this procedure with the green print borders.

Quilting suggestions

If quilting by hand, quilt in the ditch around each of the butterflies and each of the flowers. Quilt a motif in the large green triangles. Stitch in the ditch on both sides of the narrow border. Quilt a design in the green border.

If quilting by machine, machine stipple in the background behind the flowers and butterflies. Quilt a design in the green triangles, and stitch in the ditch on both sides of the narrow border. Quilt a design in the green border.

Binding

Before binding, hand-baste a scant 1/4" from the edge of the quilt.

Join the binding strips with diagonal seams pressed open and trimmed to 1/4". Sew the binding strips to the quilt with a 1/4" seam. (See page 12 for instructions on binding and mitered corners.) Trim the excess backing and batting even with the quilt top. Turn the binding over 1/4" and turn to the back side, covering the stitching. Sew down by hand with matching thread.

FLOWER BASKETS

(18" x 22", 3" block)

Tool Requirements
Easy Angle
Companion Angle

Fabric Requirements
Background: 3/8 yard
Variety of prints: 4" x 8" piece
for *each* basket
Border: 1/4 yard

Binding (for Civil War era
version): 1/8 yard

Additional Supplies
For the '30s version of *Flower
Baskets*, you will also need a
small amount of fusible webbing
and complementary colors of
embroidery floss.

I first made the '30s version of **Flower Baskets** in scraps of vintage feedsacks and house-dresses from the '30s and '40s. The baskets without the pieced triangles looked empty, so I added the star flowers with French knot centers.

Curious to see how the same pattern would look in darker fabrics, I choose a grouping of reproduction Civil War fabrics and scrappy tea-dyed background fabrics, and made all the baskets with the pieced triangle tops. The result is very different. Choose your own favorite fabrics to make **Flower Baskets.**

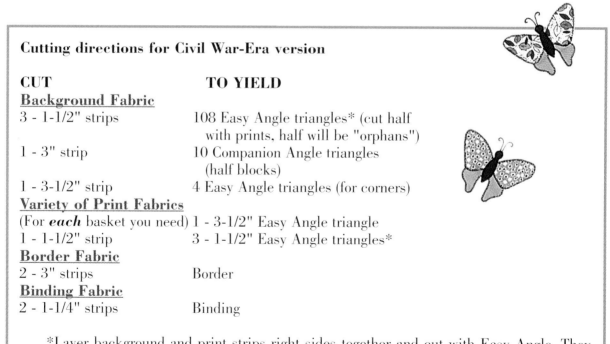

Cutting directions for Civil War-Era version

CUT	TO YIELD
Background Fabric	
3 - 1-1/2" strips	108 Easy Angle triangles* (cut half with prints, half will be "orphans")
1 - 3" strip	10 Companion Angle triangles (half blocks)
1 - 3-1/2" strip	4 Easy Angle triangles (for corners)
Variety of Print Fabrics	
(For *each* basket you need)	1 - 3-1/2" Easy Angle triangle
1 - 1-1/2" strip	3 - 1-1/2" Easy Angle triangles*
Border Fabric	
2 - 3" strips	Border
Binding Fabric	
2 - 1-1/4" strips	Binding

*Layer background and print strips right sides together and cut with Easy Angle. They will then be ready to chain sew.

NOTE: If not using Easy Angle, cut 1-7/8" and 3-7/8" squares, cutting once on the diagonal. If not using Companion Angle, cut three 6-1/4" squares, cut twice on the diagonal.

Civil War Era Version

18" x 22"

'30s Version
18" x 22"

'30s version cutting directions

<u>**Background Fabric**</u>

1 - 3-1/2" strip	6 Easy Angle triangles (basket blocks)
	4 Easy Angle triangles (corners)
1 - 3" strip	10 Companion Angle triangles (half blocks)
2 - 1-1/2" strips	72 Easy Angle triangles (cut half with prints, half will be "orphans")
1 - 2-1/2" strip	4 squares (for border corners)

<u>**Variety of Print Fabrics**</u>

(For *each* basket you need)	1 - 3-1/2" Easy Angle triangle
(For 12 baskets you will also need)	3 - 1-1/2" Easy Angle triangles
	22 star flowers

<u>**Border Fabric**</u>

2 - 2-1/2" strips	Border
2 - 1-1/4" strips	Binding

Block assembly

Assemble all the triangle squares, pressing toward the print fabric.

Make 3

Sew the triangle squares and "orphan" triangles together to form the top of the basket blocks.

Sew the two halves of the basket block together *carefully* as you have two bias edges. Press the seam toward the basket.

Join the blocks and half blocks in diagonal rows. In the '30s version, alternate plain and pieced blocks, keeping the plain blocks in the center of the quilt. Press the seams in alternating directions.

Join the diagonal rows, then add the corner squares. Press the seams all one direction.

Trim the quilt edges square, leaving a 1/4" seam allowance from the corners of the blocks.

Borders

Measure the quilt *width* through the center. Cut two borders to this *length*. Sew to the top and bottom of the quilt. Press toward the borders.

Measure the length of the quilt through the middle. Cut two borders this length and sew them to the sides of the quilt if you are making the Civil War era version. For the '30s version, cut two borders the length of the quilt (including seam allowances) *without* adding in the top and bottom borders. Sew the background squares to both ends of the borders, and then sew the borders to the sides of the quilt. Press the seams toward the border.

Embellishment (for the '30s version)

From a variety of prints, trace 22 star flowers on the paper side of fusible webbing. Roughly cut out each star. Fuse to the wrong side of the fabrics, then cut out on the marked line. Peel off the paper and fuse the star flowers in place on the baskets. Also fuse a star flower in each corner of the quilt. French knots made with two strands of embroidery floss in various colors accent the center of the flowers. This can be done before quilting or after the quilt is completed.

Quilting suggestions

Quilt, by hand or machine, in the ditch in the seams joining the blocks. Also stitch between the bottom and top of the baskets (you can stitch this in horizontal rows across the quilt). If desired, a design can be quilted in the half blocks and outside border.

Binding

Before binding, hand-baste a scant 1/4" from the edge of the quilt.

Join the binding strips with diagonal seams pressed open and trimmed to 1/4". Sew the binding strips to the quilt with a 1/4" seam. (See page 12 for instructions on binding and mitered corners.) Trim the excess backing and batting even with the quilt top. Turn binding under 1/4", turn to the back side, covering the stitching line. Sew down by hand with matching thread.

JACOB'S LADDER

(16" x 20", 4" block)

Tool Requirement
Easy Angle

Fabric Requirements
Red solid: 1/4 yard
Light print: 1/4 yard
Red print: 1/4 yard
Dark blue print: 1/4 yard

Cutting directions

CUT	TO YIELD
Red Solid Fabric	
3 - 2-1/2" strips	24 Easy Angle triangles * Borders
Light Print Fabric	
1 - 2-1/2" strip	24 Easy Angle triangles *
Red Print Fabric	
2 - 1-1/2" strips	4 patches
Dark Blue Print Fabric	
2 - 1-1/2" strips	4 patches
2 - 1-1/4" strips	Binding

   *Layer red solid and light print strips right sides together and cut with Easy Angle. They will then be ready to chain sew.

   NOTE: If not using Easy Angle, cut 2-7/8" squares. Cut once on the diagonal.

Block assembly

Assemble all the triangle squares and press toward the red triangle.

Make 24

Sew the two different 1-1/2" print strips together. Press toward the dark blue strips. Cut into fifty-six 1-1/2" units.

Cut into 56, 1-1/2" units

Sew two units together to form four patches. Make 28. Press.

 Make 28

Sew four-patch blocks and triangle square units together in rows of six, alternating the blocks and the orientation of the red triangles. Place all the four-patch units the same way, so you achieve a "chain effect."

The *Jacob's Ladder* block can be arranged in many interesting ways. Try different layouts for the units, and design your own quilt!

Borders

Measure and cut borders the exact length and width of the quilt. Sew the borders to the top and bottom of the quilt and press. Sew the extra four-patches to both ends of the side borders. Sew to the sides of the quilt and press.

Quilting suggestions

Quilt by hand or machine in the ditch following the diagonal lines of the triangle squares. Run a line of quilting on the opposite diagonal through the center of the triangle squares. Stitch a design in the border.

Binding

Before binding, hand baste a scant 1/4" from the edge of the quilt.

Join the binding strips with diagonal seams pressed open and trimmed to 1/4". Sew the binding strips to the quilt with a 1/4" seam. (See page 12 for instructions on binding and mitered corners.) Trim the excess backing and batting even with the quilt top. Turn binding under 1/4", turn to the back side, covering the stitching line. Sew down by hand with matching thread.

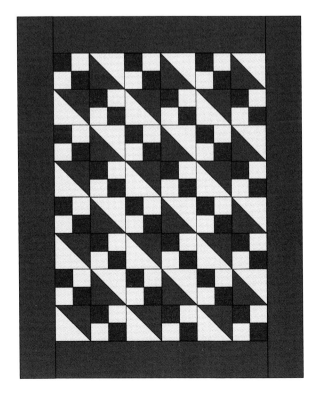

MINIATURE PINK TULIPS

(15-1/2" square, 3-1/2" block)

A variegated pink fabric was used for the tulips, which allowed me to cut all the pieces from one fabric, just adding light or dark contrasting squares for the center of the tulips. If your pink fabric is a solid color (or a print that reads like a solid), choose a contrasting fabric for the tulip centers.

Tool Requirement
Tri-Recs

Fabric Requirements
Pink: 1/4 yard
Darker pink: scraps or 1/4 yard
White tone-on-tone: 1/2 yard
Medium green print: 1/4 yard
Darker green accent: scraps

15-1/2" Square

Tulip blocks

Right sides together, sew the white Recs triangles to pink Recs triangles, using the cut-off tip for alignment. Press toward the colored fabric. Make 96 units.

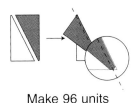

Make 96 units

Layer the white and dark pink 1" strips right sides together. Sew, press and cut into forty-eight 1" x 1-1/2" rectangles.

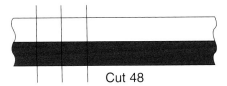

Cut 48

Sew the 1" x 1-1/2" white rectangles to the rectangles you have created with the dark pink and white squares. Press toward the white rectangle.

For each tulip, you will need a pair of Recs units, both a right and a left side, a matching square for the base of the tulip, and a contrasting center square unit. Assemble as shown, following pressing arrows.

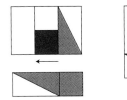

Join 22 pairs of tulips with the white sashing strips. Press toward the sashing.

Add the green square between 18 of the remaining white sashing strips. Press toward the sashing strips.

Assemble 9 tulip blocks. Press toward the sashing.

Set the tulip blocks 3 x 3, using the green sashing strips with darker green stepping stones. Press toward the sashing.

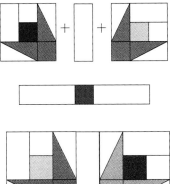

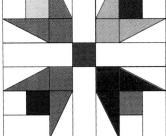

Make 9

Inside border

Measure and cut 4 green borders the exact width of the quilt. Sew a border to the top and bottom of the quilt. Press toward the borders.

Sew dark green corner squares to both ends of the remaining borders. Press toward the borders. Sew to the sides of the quilt. Press toward the borders.

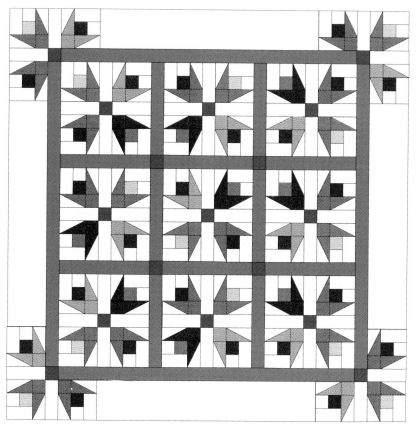

Quilting suggestions

Quilt by hand or machine in the ditch on both sides of the tulip blocks, the sashing and inside border. Quilt an interesting design in the long white border.

Binding

Before binding, hand baste a scant 1/4" from the edge of the quilt.

Join the binding strips with diagonal seams pressed open and trimmed to 1/4". Sew the binding strips to the quilt with a 1/4" seam. (See page 12 for instructions on binding and mitered corners.) Trim the excess backing and batting even with the quilt top. Turn binding under 1/4", turn to the back side, covering the stitching line. Sew down by hand with matching thread.

Pieced border

To two of the white 2" x 9" borders, add the single tulips, facing toward the center. Add 2" white sashing strips at the ends of both of these borders. Add the borders to two sides of the quilt. Press the seam toward the green inside border.

Join the pairs of tulips to both ends of the remaining two white borders. Press the seams toward the borders. Sew the borders to the quilt. Press the seam toward the green inside border.

SCRAPPY DELIGHT
(and variation)

(7" x 9", 2" block)

This sweet little quilt uses a large variety of scraps. The pattern is given in two different sizes, and two colorations, which can be quickly machine quilted. This is a wonderfully simple project in either size, and is a great way to use some of those leftover fabrics! If each of the stars is made from different fabrics, you'll create a charm quilt.

Tool Requirements
Easy Angle
Companion Angle

Fabric Requirements
Scraps of background and dark prints
Border and binding: 1/4 yard

7" x 9"

Cutting directions

For **each** star you will need:

1 - 1-1/2" square for the center

8 Easy Angle triangles cut from a 1" strip for the star points

4 - 1" squares of background fabric

4 Companion Angle triangles, cut from a 1" strip of background fabric.

NOTE: If not using Easy Angle, cut 1-3/8" squares. Cut once on the diagonal for the star points.

If not using Companion Angle, cut 2-1/4" squares. Cut twice on the diagonal for the background triangles that fit between the star points.

Star blocks

Add the small print triangles to both sides of the larger background triangle, making "flying geese" units. Press.

Make 24 (36)

Make 24 (36)

Sew two flying geese units to opposite sides of the print square. Press toward the square.

Add the background squares to both ends of the remaining geese units. Press toward the squares.

Make 6 (9)

Make 12 (18)

Join the three units to form a star. Press toward the large square.

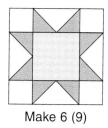

Make 6 (9)

Border

From the border print, cut a strip 1-3/4" wide. Measure and cut two borders the exact *width* of the quilt. Sew to the top and bottom of the quilt. Press the seams toward the borders.

Measure and cut two borders the exact *length* of the quilt. Sew to the sides of the quilt. Press the seams toward the borders.

Quilting suggestions

Machine or hand quilt in the ditch between the blocks and between the blocks and the border.

Binding

Before binding, hand baste a scant 1/4" from the edge of the quilt.

Join the binding strips with diagonal seams pressed open and trimmed to 1/4". Sew the binding strips to the quilt with a 1/4" seam. (See page 12 for instructions on binding and mitered corners.) Trim the excess backing and batting even with the quilt top. Turn binding under 1/4", turn to the back side, covering the stitching line. Sew down by hand with matching thread.

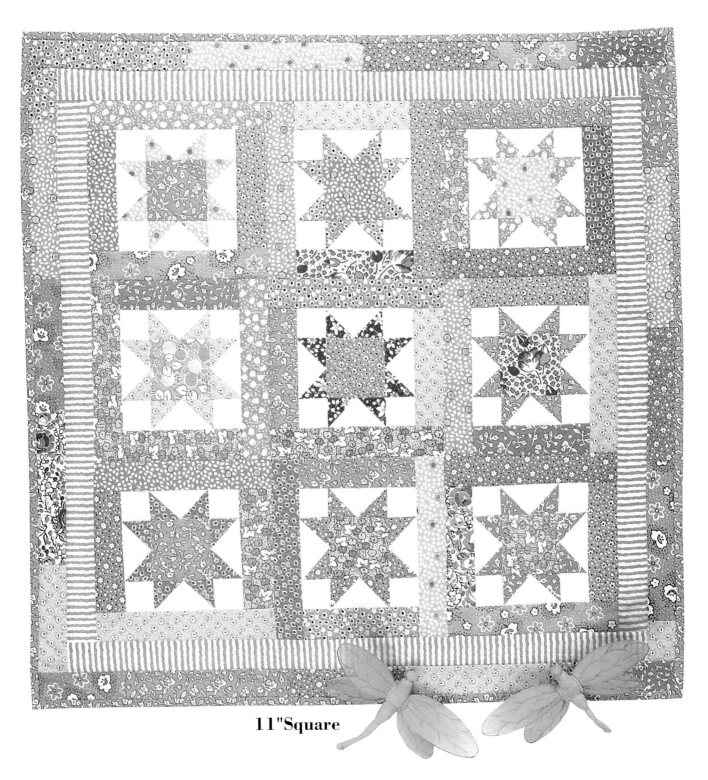

11"Square

'30s version of Scrappy Stars

Cut out and assemble the star blocks using the directions on page 72. When the star blocks are finished, cut 18 sashes from a variety of prints measuring 1" x 2-1/2". Sew to the top and bottom of the blocks. Cut 18 sashes from a variety of prints measuring 1" x 3-1/2". Sew to the sides of the blocks. Join the blocks in three rows of three, alternating them top to bottom, side to side (so the sashing seams all alternate). Cut an inside striped border strip 1" wide, sew to the quilt. Then add either a 2" cut border of a print, or print strips 1" wide and random lengths.

Finish, following the directions on previous page.

SCRAPPY DELIGHT II

(16" square, 4" block)

Tool Requirements
Easy Angle
Companion Angle

Fabric Requirements
Background: 1/4 yard or a variety of scraps
Prints: scraps
Border and binding: 1/4 yard

Cutting directions
For *each* star cut:
1 2-1/2" print square for the center
8 Easy Angle triangles cut from a 1-1/2" print strip for star points
4 squares and 4 Companion Angle triangles cut from a 1-1/2" strip of background fabric.

NOTE: If not using Easy Angle, cut 1-7/8" squares. Cut once on the diagonal for the star points.

If not using Companion Angle, cut 3-1/4" squares. Cut twice on the diagonal for the background triangles that fit between the star points.

Star blocks

Add the small print triangles to both sides of the larger background triangle, making "flying geese" units. Press.

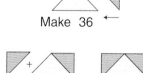

Make 36

Make 36

Sew two flying geese units to opposite sides of the print square. Press toward the square.

Make 9

Add the background squares to both ends of the remaining geese units. Press toward the squares.

Make 18

Join the three units to form a star. Press toward the large square.

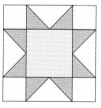

Make 9

Border

Cut two strips 2-1/2" wide. Cut two borders the exact *width* of the quilt. Sew to the top and bottom of the quilt. Press the seams toward the borders.

Cut two borders the exact *length* of the quilt. Sew to the sides of the quilt and press the seams toward the borders.

Quilting suggestions

Quilt in the ditch around each of the star blocks. Quilt in the ditch between the blocks. Stitch on both sides of the striped border.

Binding

Before binding, hand-baste a scant 1/4" from the edge of the quilt.

Join the binding strips with diagonal seams pressed open and trimmed to 1/4". Sew the binding strips to the quilt with a 1/4" seam. (See page 12 for instructions on binding and mitered corners.) Trim the excess backing and batting even with the quilt top. Turn binding under 1/4", turn to the back side, covering the stitching line. Sew down by hand with matching thread.

16" Square

SWEETHEARTS

(21" square, 3-1/2" block)

"Sweethearts" is a sweet and romantic miniature quilt. You could embellish the appliquéd hearts with beads, lace or other trims for an even more Victorian look. Wouldn't this be the perfect quilt for a daughter (or daughter-in-law) or granddaughter? Perhaps you would like to make one for yourself!

Tool Requirement
Easy Angle

Fabric Requirements
Background: 1/3 yard
Dark pink for bows: 1/4 yard
Light pink for hearts: scraps
Medium green for sashing and bias binding: 1/2 yard
Dark green for corner squares: scraps
Large print for border: 1/3 yard (If you choose a vertical stripe like mine, then you need 2/3 yard)

CUT	TO YIELD
Background Fabric	
1 - 4" strip	4 squares
1 - 1-1/2" strip	10 squares
	15 rectangles 1" x 1-1/2"
3 - 1" strips	5 rectangles 1" x 2-1/2"
	50 squares
	50 Easy Angle triangles*
Dark Pink Fabric	
3 - 1" strips	20 1" x 2" rectangles
	50 Easy Angle triangles*
	35 squares
Light Pink Fabric	
4 hearts	

CUT	TO YIELD
Medium Green Fabric	
3 - 1" strips	12 - 1" x 4" sashes
	Inside border
1-1/4" bias strips	Binding
Dark Green Fabric	
1" strip	4 squares (for corner stones)
Large Print Fabric	
2 - 4-1/2" strips	Outside border

   NOTE: If not using Easy Angle, cut squares 1-3/8". Cut once on the diagonal.
   *Layer pink and background right sides together and cut with Easy Angle. They will then be ready to chain-sew.

Quilt assembly

   Assemble all the triangle squares and press toward the darker fabric.

   Sew the background squares to both sides of the dark pink rectangles. Mark a diagonal line on each square and sew on the diagonal lines. Trim the seam allowance to 1/4" and press the seams toward the dark rectangle.

Make 50

Make 20

The blocks are assembled in sections, and most are mirror images of one another. You need to make five units like this:

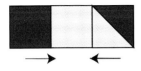

Make five units like this:

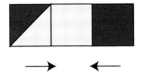

Make five units like this:

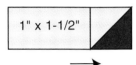

Make five units like this:

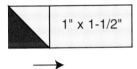

Make five units like this:

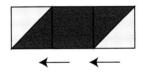

Make five units like this:

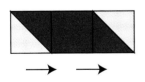

Make five units like this: And five like this:

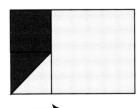   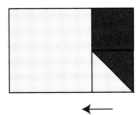

21" Square

You need to make five units to join the two sides of the bow:

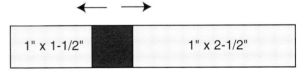

Make 5

After assembling all the units, join the units to make complete bow blocks. Press.

Congratulations! Your block is finished—yes, it still looks odd, but after the sashings are added, it will be fine.

Appliqué the four hearts on the plain blocks, using whichever method you prefer (see pages 15-16 for more information on appliqué).

Lay out the blocks, alternating hearts and bows. Add sashing between the blocks, with the dark green squares as corner stones between the sashings.

Borders

Measure and cut two medium green borders the *width* of the quilt. Sew to the top and bottom of the quilt. Press the seams toward the borders.

Measure and cut two medium green borders the *length* of the quilt. Sew to the sides of the quilt. Press the seams toward the borders.

Add the wider large print borders in the same manner.

Scalloped border

To mark the scalloped edge, make a template out of paper. Cut a piece of paper the same length as the quilt. Take the measurement of the quilt and divide the side measurement evenly by 3, 4 or 5 (the number of scallops desired). Make a mark along the edge of the paper at these intervals. At each of these marks, measure in 1", and then make a second mark directly below the first mark at the edge of the paper. Using a small plate or bowl from your kitchen of the right diameter, mark a smooth curve connecting the second set of marks. At the corners, the curves should overlap so that the corner comes to more of a point. Experiment until it looks right. Once you have the paper pattern drawn out to your satisfaction, cut it out carefully with a scissors. Open the paper pattern and make any adjustments you feel are necessary on the paper. When you are satisfied with the scalloped border, pin it to the quilt top and mark the scallop on the right side of the quilt with a quilt chalk pencil or quilt marker. **Do not cut** this scallop until you have the binding sewn on. (This will keep the edge from stretching and distorting.) Use the chalk line as a sewing guide when you add the bias binding.

Quilting suggestions

Hand or machine quilt in the ditch inside each of the blocks. Quilt around the hearts. Quilt in the ditch between the green inside border and the wide outside border. Quilt a design in the border, using parallel lines, cross-hatching or a large machine meander.

Binding

NOTE: Before binding, hand-baste just inside the chalk marking of the scalloped edge. This prevents the edge from distorting as the binding is sewn on. The scalloped edge of this quilt needs to be finished with a *bias* binding cut 1-1/4" wide from medium green. The bias binding will go smoothly around the curves, and is used singly to reduce the bulk at the inside corners.

Begin at the top of a curve with the binding cut at a 45-degree angle and folded over 1/4". Stitch a 1/4" seam with the edge of the binding at the chalk marking. When you come to the inside of each curve, stop with the needle down, lift the pressure foot, pivot, and pull the binding into position. Keeping it flat under the needle, lower the pressure foot and continue sewing. Avoid stitching any pleats in that corner. You will have excess fabric in that inside curve until you fold it to the back side, then it will fold in upon itself like a reverse mitered corner. Continue around the quilt until you return to the starting point. Then simply overlap the beginning by 1", cutting off the excess binding at a 45-degree angle.

Trim off the excess batting and backing at the chalk marking. Fold the binding under 1/4", then over to the back side of the quilt, covering the stitching, and stitch down by hand. It is not necessary to clip at the inside curves. The excess fabric folds nicely over itself like a mitered corner.

RED HOTS

(12-1/4" x 16-1/2", 3" blocks)

This little Americana quilt reminded me of the red hot candies that would be tucked into Valentine's cards when I was young. Remember? They look so deceptively innocent until you hold them in your mouth for awhile! In the same manner, this quilt uses a simple star but makes a great impact.

Tool Requirement
Companion Angle

Fabric Requirements
Background: 1/4 yard
Red print: 1/4 yard
Plaid: 1/4 yard
Navy print: 1/4 yard

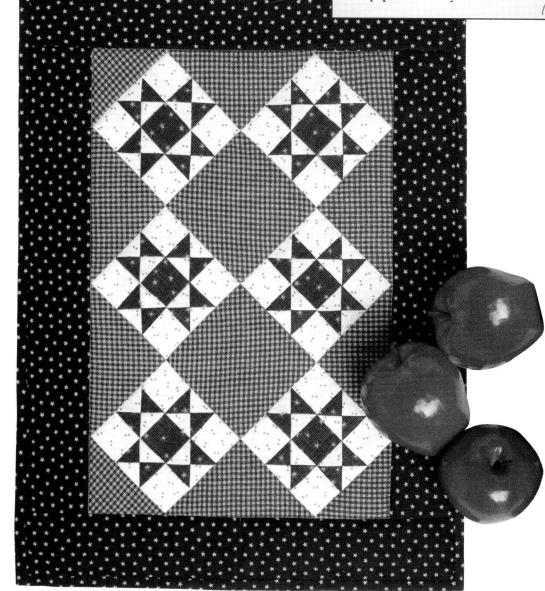

12-1/4" x 16-1/2"

Cutting directions

CUT	TO YIELD
Background Fabric	
1 - 1-1/2" strip	24 squares
2 - 1" strips	48 Companion Angle triangles*
Red Fabric	
1 - 1-1/2" strip	6 squares
2 - 1" strips	48 Companion Angle triangles*
Plaid Fabric	
2 - 3-1/2" squares cut on the bias	
2 - 3-1/2" squares cut on the straight, and cut once on the diagonal for 4 corners	
1 - 2-3/4" strip	6 Companion angle triangles (for half blocks)
Navy Print Fabric	
2 - 2-1/4" strips	Borders
2 - 1-1/4" strips	Binding

*Layer the background and red print fabrics right sides together and cut with Companion Angle. They are then ready to chain sew.

NOTE: If not using Companion Angle, cut twelve 2-1/4" squares for the small triangles. Cut twice on the diagonal. For the half blocks, cut two 5-3/4" squares. Cut twice on the diagonal.

Quilt assembly

Make 48

Make 24

Chain-sew all the small Companion Angle triangles together, having the red print on top. Sew on the right-hand side of the triangle each time. Press toward the red triangle.

Join the units to make 24 Broken Dishes blocks.

Assemble six star blocks. Assemble the quilt top in diagonal rows, using the plaid plain blocks and half and corner blocks. (*NOTE:* The side and corner triangles are slightly larger than needed.) Press and trim square.

Make 6

Borders

Measure and cut two borders the *width* of the quilt. Sew to the top and bottom of the quilt. Press the seams toward the borders.

Measure and cut two borders the *length* of the quilt. Sew to the sides of the quilt. Press the seams toward the borders.

Quilting suggestions

Quilt by hand or by machine in the ditch around each of the blocks. Quilt in the ditch around the center red square in each star block, and quilt a simple design in the plain whole, half and corner blocks, or machine stipple in those same areas. Quilt in the ditch just inside the border. The border may be left unquilted or a simple design may be added.

Binding

Before binding, hand-baste a scant 1/4" from the edge of the quilt.

Join the binding strips with diagonal seams pressed open and trimmed to 1/4". Sew the binding strips to the quilt with a 1/4" seam. (See page 12 for instructions on binding and mitered corners.) Trim the excess backing and batting even with the quilt top. Turn binding under 1/4", turn to the back side, covering the stitching line. Sew down by hand with matching thread.

SHOOT FOR THE STARS

(12-1/4" x 15-1/4")

Tool Requirements
Easy Angle
Companion Angle

Fabric Requirements
Background: 1/3 yard
Gold: scraps
Black with gold stars: 1/4 yard
Two coordinating scraps for each rocket (6 rockets)

Make this quilt just for fun or for the little boy (or big boy) in your life who is a space enthusiast. The quilt assembles quickly and easily, especially if you refer to the piecing diagrams, which illustrate how all the pieces fit together.

12-1/4" x 15-1/4"

Cutting directions for rockets

CUT	TO YIELD
Background Fabric	
2 - 1-1/2" strips	12 rectangles 1-1/2" x 3-1/2"
	6 rectangles 1" x 1-1/2"
2 - 1" strips	12 rectangles 1" x 2"
	6 rectangles 1" x 2-1/2" (fins)
	24 - 1" squares
Each **main body of rocket**	
	1 - 1-1/2" x 2-1/2" rectangle
Each **set of nose and fins**	
1 - 1" strip	1 - 1" x 1-1/2" rectangle (nose)
	2 rectangles 1" x 2-1/2" (fins)
	2 - 1" squares

Assembly directions for rocket blocks

Mark a diagonal line on two background squares. Place the square on top of the "nose" rectangle. Sew on the diagonal line, trim the seam allowance to 1/4", and press toward the "nose" of the rocket. Repeat at the opposite corner. Press.

Make 6

Assemble the top part of the rocket as shown. Press the seams toward the rocket.

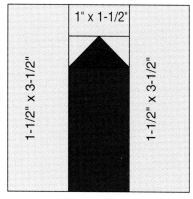

1" x 1-1/2"

1-1/2" x 3-1/2"

1-1/2" x 3-1/2"

Make 6

Assemble the top and bottom part of the fins by placing a square over the rectangle, and sewing on the diagonal as you did for the rocket nose. Press toward the rocket each time.

1" x 2-1/2"

Make 6 each

Assemble the bottom section of the rocket as shown. Press the seams toward the rocket.

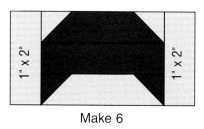

1" x 2"

1" x 2"

Make 6

Assemble the rockets in two rows, with three rockets in each row.

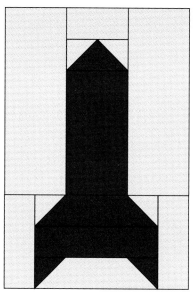

Make 6

Cutting directions for large stars

CUT	TO YIELD
Background Fabric	
1 - 1-1/2" strip	8 squares
	3 sashings 1-1/2" x 3-1/2"
1 - 1" strip	8 Companion Angle triangles*
Gold Fabric	
1 - 1-1/2" strip	8 Easy Angle triangles
Black Fabric	
	2 - 1-1/2" squares
1 - 1" strip	8 Companion Angle triangles*

*Layer background and black strips right sides together and cut with Companion Angle. They will then be ready to chain-sew.

NOTE: If not using Easy Angle, cut 1-7/8" squares. Cut once on the diagonal.

If not using Companion Angle, cut 2-1/4" squares. Cut twice on the diagonal.

Assembly directions for large star blocks

With right sides together, sew the Companion Angle triangles together on the right-hand side, having the light triangle on the top. Press toward the dark triangle.

Make 8

Add each of these units to the larger gold triangles. Press toward the large triangle.

Assemble two star blocks.

Make 8

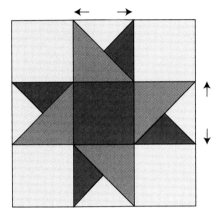

Add sashing strips between the stars and on both sides of the stars. Sew the star section to the top of the rocket section.

Cutting directions for *Friendship Stars* and borders

CUT	TO YIELD
Background Fabric	
1 - 1" strip	16 squares
	16 Easy Angle triangles*
Gold Fabric	
1 - 1" strip	4 squares
	16 Easy Angle triangles*
Black Fabric	
2 - 2" strips	Borders
2 - 1-1/4" strips	Binding

*Layer background and gold fabrics right sides together and cut with Easy Angle. They will then be ready to chain-sew. **NOTE:** If not using Easy Angle, cut 1-3/8" squares. Cut once on the diagonal.

Borders

Sew all the triangle squares and press toward the darker fabric. Assemble four *Friendship Stars* for the corners of the quilt.

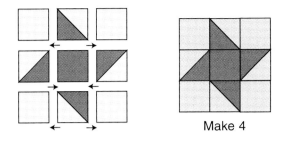

Make 4

Measure and cut the side, top, and bottom borders to the exact measurements of your quilt.

Sew the top and bottom borders to the quilt. Press toward the borders.

Sew the *Friendship Stars* to both ends of the side borders and press. Sew to the sides of the quilt. Press the seams toward the side borders.

Quilting suggestions

Machine meander in the background area behind the rockets. Stitch two parallel rows of quilting down the length of each rocket. Stitch in the ditch around the center square in each of the large stars. Quilt in the ditch inside the border.

Binding

Before binding, hand baste a scant 1/4" from the edge of the quilt.

Join the binding strips with diagonal seams pressed open and trimmed to 1/4". Sew the binding strips to the quilt with a 1/4" seam. (See page 12 for instructions on binding and mitered corners.) Trim the excess backing and batting even with the quilt top. Turn binding under 1/4", turn to the back side, covering the stitching line. Sew down by hand with matching thread.

SMALL SINGLE WEDDING RING
(8-1/2" x 13-3/4", 2-1/2" block)

CUT   TO YIELD

Background Fabric
3 - 1" strips 54 squares
              72 Easy Angle triangles*
1 - 3" strip 2 - 3" squares
              4 Easy Angle triangles
              (for corners)
              6 Companion Angle triangles
              (for half blocks)

Sueded Cottons (from _each_ fabric cut)
1 - 1" strip 2 - 1" squares
              2 - 1" x 2" rectangles
              12 Easy Angle triangles*

Print Fabric
1 - 2" strip Border
2 - 1-1/4" strips
              Binding

  *Layer background and sueded cottons right sides together and cut. They are then ready to chain-sew.
  NOTE: If not using Easy Angle, cut 1-3/8" squares for the small triangle squares. Cut once on the diagonal. For the corner triangles, cut two 3" squares once on the diagonal.
  If not using Companion Angle, cut two 6-1/4" squares. Cut twice on the diagonal.

Block assembly

  Assemble all the triangle squares first. Press and trim "dog-ears."
  Assemble 12 rows, press as directed.

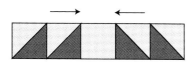

Make 12

Place a background square on one end of a 1" x 2" dark rectangle. Stitch on the diagonal of the square. Trim seam to 1/4". Press. Repeat on the opposite corner.

Make 12

Tool Requirements
Easy Angle
Companion Angle

Fabric Requirements
Background: 1/4 yard
Scraps of hand-dyed sueded cottons*
Print for border and binding: 1/4 yard

* Sueded hand-dyed fabrics are available from Cherrywood Fabrics, Inc. P.O. Box 486, Brainerd, MN 56401-0486. (1-888-298-0967).

  Add a triangle square on each end of the pieced rectangle. Press as directed.

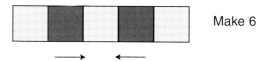

Make 12

  Assemble six rows of squares. Press as directed.

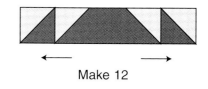

Make 6

  Join all the rows to form six _Wedding Ring_ blocks. Press toward the center of each block.

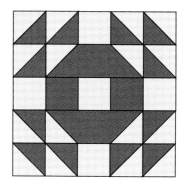

Make 6

Quilt assembly

Set the blocks on point. Add the plain squares in the center, and the setting triangles on the outside edges. Use the large Easy Angle triangles for the corners. (**NOTE:** The setting triangles are cut larger than needed.) Join the blocks and setting triangles in diagonal rows. Press. Join the rows. Press the top, then trim, allowing 1/4" seam allowances around the outside.

Borders

Measure and cut two borders the *width* of the quilt. Sew to the top and bottom of the quilt. Press toward the borders.

Measure and cut two borders the *length* of the quilt. Sew to the sides of the quilt. Press toward the borders.

Quilting suggestions

By hand, quilt an interesting motif in each of the plain blocks, and half of that same motif in each of the setting triangles. Quilt in the ditch around the center square in the pieced block, and quilt a design in the border.

If you'd rather machine quilt, a small meander around the piecing and in the outside border would highlight the pieced blocks.

Binding

Before binding, hand-baste a scant 1/4" from the edge of the quilt.

Join the binding strips with diagonal seams pressed open and trimmed to 1/4". Sew the binding strips to the quilt with a 1/4" seam. (See page 12 for instructions on binding and mitered corners.) Trim the excess backing and batting even with the quilt top. Turn binding under 1/4", turn to the back side, covering the stitching line. Sew down by hand with matching thread.

8-1/2" x 13-3/4"

LARGE WEDDING RING

(24-1/2" square, 5" block)

Tool Requirement	Fabric Requirements
Easy Angle	Background: 3/8 yard of hand-dyed sueded cotton*
	Solids: small pieces of five different solids in the sueded cotton
	Black: 1/3 yard
	Print: 1/2 yard

*Hand-dyed sueded cottons are available from Cherrywood Fabrics, P. O. Box 486, Brainerd, MN 56401-0486; (888-298-0967).

CUT	TO YIELD	CUT	TO YIELD
Background Fabric		**From One Solid**	
4 - 1-1/2" strips	45 squares	4 - 1" squares for	corner squares
	60 Easy Angle triangles*	**Black Fabric**	
1 - 5" strip	2 squares, cut diagonally for corner triangles	5 - 1" strips	4 - 1" x 6-1/2"
			12 - 1" x 5-1/2"
	4 Companion Angle triangles (for half blocks)		Inside Border
		3 - 1-1/4" strips	Binding
Solids: From *each* fabric cut		**Print Fabric**	
1 - 1-1/2" strip	2 squares	3 - 4" strips	Outside border
	12 Easy Angle triangles*		
	2 - 1-1/2" x 3-1/2" rectangles		

*Layer 1-1/2" background and solid fabric strips right sides together and cut 12 Easy Angle triangles. They will then be ready to chain sew.

NOTE: If not using Easy Angle, cut 1-7/8" squares. Cut once on the diagonal.

If not using Companion Angle, cut 1, 10-1/4" square. Cut twice on the diagonal.

Assemble the blocks according to the directions given in the *Single Wedding Ring* miniature pattern. Set the blocks on point, adding sashing strips and corner stones between the blocks, and using the triangles for the corners and half blocks.

Trim the quilt square, leaving 1/4" seam allowance.

24-1/2" Square

Borders

Measure and cut two narrow black borders the *width* of the quilt. Sew to the top and bottom of the quilt and press toward the borders.

Measure and cut two narrow black borders the *length* of the quilt. Sew to the sides of the quilt and press toward the borders.

Add the wider print border in the same manner.

Quilting suggestions

With matching or contrasting thread, by hand or machine, quilt in the ditch around each block. Also, quilt in the ditch inside and outside of the center portion of each block, or just a single line of quilting 1/4" from the edge of the center "ring." Quilt a grid in the plain half and corner blocks. Quilt in the ditch inside both borders. A design, cross-hatching, or parallel lines may be quilted in the border.

Binding

Before binding, hand baste a scant 1/4" from the edge of the quilt.

Join the binding strips with diagonal seams pressed open and trimmed to 1/4". Sew the binding strips to the quilt with a 1/4" seam. (See page 12 for instructions on binding and mitered corners.) Trim the excess backing and batting even with the quilt top. Turn binding under 1/4", turn to the back side, covering the stitching line. Sew down by hand with matching thread.

SOMETHING'S FISHY
(20" x 22")

Cutting directions

Cut the borders for the quilt before cutting the rest of the pieces. Since water prints tend to be directional, it might be best to cut the side borders the *length* of the fabric.

Cut two 2-1/2" borders 24" long *along the selvage of the fabric*. These will be your side borders. Cut one 2-1/2" strip for the top and bottom border across the width of your remaining fabric. Set the border aside for later.

Tool Requirements
Tri-Recs
Easy Angle
Companion Angle

Fabric Requirements
Blue water fabric: 1 yard
Assorted bright colors: fat quarters
Orange solid: 1/4 yard

Additional Requirements
Buttons or beads for eyes

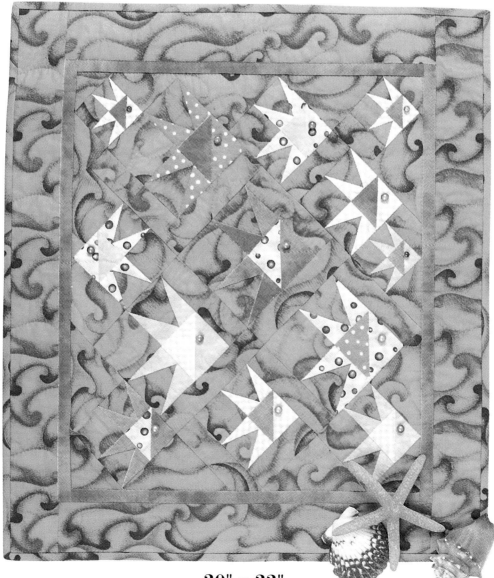

20" x 22"

CUT	TO YIELD
<u>Blue Water Fabric</u>	
1 - 2-1/2" strip	4 squares
	8 Tri pieces (for 4 large fish)
1 - 2" strip	6 squares
	12 Tri pieces (for 6 medium fish)
1 - 1-1/2" strip	3 squares
	6 Tri pieces (for 3 small fish)
<u>Various Bright Fabrics</u>	
1 - 2-1/2" strip	for large fish
1 - 2" strip	for medium fish
1 - 1-1/2" strip	for small fish

For each fish, cut two different bright Easy Angle triangles for the body, and two bright *pairs* of Recs pieces. You will need to cut pieces for four large fish, six medium fish, and three small fish. (*NOTE:* Using the strip sizes given above will yield the different size units.)

NOTE: If not using Easy Angle, cut 2-7/8", 2-3/8" and 1-7/8" squares, cutting once on the diagonal.

There is no easy way to cut the Tri-Recs pieces without the tools.

Block assembly

Sew a Recs piece to the right hand side of a blue water Tri piece. Press the seam toward the smaller triangle.

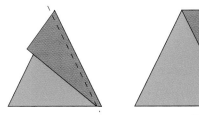
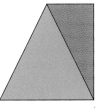

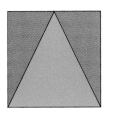

Sew the second Recs pieces to the left side of the unit and press toward the smaller triangle. Make all your Tri-Recs units in the same manner.

Sew the Easy Angle triangles together on the long edge. Press to one side and trim "dog ears."

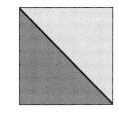

Join the four block units.

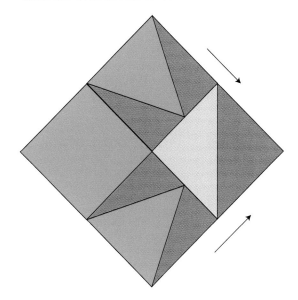

Cutting directions for sashings and setting triangles

CUT	TO YIELD
<u>Blue Water Fabric</u>	
2 - 1-1/2" strips	3 - 1-1/2" x 5-1/2" sashing
	6 - 1-1/2" x 4-1/2" sashing
	2 - 1-1/2" x 3-1/2" sashing
	2 - 1-1/2" x 2-1/2" sashing
1 - 3" strip	2 Easy Angle triangles (A)
trim strip to 2-3/4"	9 Companion Angle triangles (a)
1 - 2-1/2" strip	2 Easy Angle triangles (B)
trim strip to 2"	3 Companion Angle triangles (b)

NOTE: If not using Easy Angle, cut 3-3/8" and 2-7/8" squares, cut once on the diagonal.

If not using Companion Angle, cut 5-3/4" and 4-1/4" squares, cut twice on the diagonal.

Assembling the quilt

Following the diagram of the quilt, add the sashes around the fish blocks as indicated. Press.

Lay out the entire quilt, adding the triangles around the edges as indicated. Sew the blocks together in the units indicated in the diagram, matching seam allowances as shown. Note the outside triangles are slightly larger than needed, and in two places the sashing extends beyond the setting triangles.

Sew the large units together and press. Trim the quilt edges square, leaving at least a 1/4" seam allowance.

Borders

From the orange solid, cut two 1" strips. Measure and cut two strips the *width* of the quilt. Sew to the top and bottom of the quilt and press toward the borders.

Measure and cut two strips the *length* of the quilt. Sew to the sides of the quilt and press toward the borders.

Using the borders cut and set aside earlier, measure and cut two blue border strips the *width* of the quilt. Sew to the top and bottom of the quilt. Press toward the borders.

Using the two blue border strips cut and set aside earlier, measure and cut two borders the *length* of the quilt. Sew to the sides of the quilt and press toward the borders.

Quilting suggestion

Stitch in the ditch around each of the fish. Quilt swirls, ripples or bubbles into the background and borders. Stitch in the ditch on both sides of the orange narrow border.

Binding

Before binding, hand baste a scant 1/4" from the edge of the quilt.

Cut two 1-1/4" strips of blue water fabric. Join the binding strips with diagonal seams pressed open and trimmed to 1/4". Sew the binding strips to the quilt with a 1/4" seam. (See page 12 for instructions on binding and mitered corners.) Trim the excess backing and batting even with the quilt top. Turn binding under 1/4", turn to the back side, covering the stitching line. Sew down by hand with matching thread.

Embellishment

Add button or bead eyes to the fish.

SMALL STARS AND STRIPES

(9" x 11")

Tool Requirement
Easy Angle

Fabric Requirements
Scraps of red print, navy star print, gold print, tone-on-tone background in cream or white, red solid, navy plaid for border, and navy solid for binding.

This is a great little quilt to make for the Fourth of July, or to display all year around with an Americana collection of antiques. A new technique is taught to help you make accurate and very narrow stripes on the flags.

9" x 11"

Cutting directions

CUT   **TO YIELD**

STARS

Background Fabric

3 - 1" strips   40 squares
         8 rectangles 1" x 1-1/2"
         52 Easy Angle triangles*

Red Print Fabric

1 - 1" strip   4 squares
         16 Easy Angle triangles*

Gold Print Fabric

1 - 1" strip   4 squares
         16 Easy Angle triangles*

Navy Print Fabric

1 - 1" strip   5 squares
         20 Easy Angle triangles*

*Layer background and print fabrics right sides together and cut with Easy Angle. They will then be ready to chain sew.

NOTE: If not using Easy Angle, cut squares 1-3/8". Cut once on the diagonal.

FLAGS

Navy Star Print Fabric

1 - 1-1/4" strip   4 squares

Background Fabric for Flags

         1 - 3/4" strip

Red Solid Fabric

         2 - 3/4" strips

BORDER AND BINDING

Navy Plaid Fabric

2 - 2-1/4" x 6" (or width of center of quilt)
2 - 3" x 6" (or length of center of quilt)

Navy Solid Fabric

1 - 1-1/4" strip   Binding

Assembling the stars

Assemble all the triangle squares; press and trim off the "dog ears." The stars are a simple 9-patch. Assemble only the red and navy stars according to the diagram, following the pressing directions:

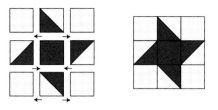

Make 5 navy
Make 4 red

The gold stars are part of the sashing that divides the stars. Add the gold triangle squares to the rectangles, turning the points the correct way. Assemble two rows with navy star— red star—navy star, and one row with red star—navy star—red star.

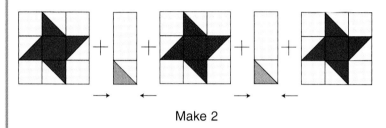

Make 2

Assemble two sashing strips that fit between the star rows:

Press, following the pressing arrows. Join all the rows.

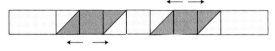

Make 2

Assembling the flags

Sew the narrow strips of red and white together carefully. Refer to page 10-11 for instruction on how to piece very narrow borders. Press the seams toward the red fabric. Cut the strips into eight pieces that measure 3" long, and four pieces that measure 2-1/4" long.

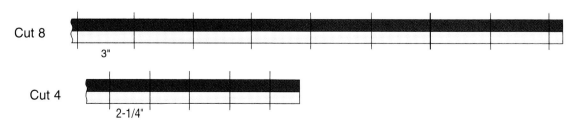

Cut 8

3"

Cut 4

2-1/4"

Make 4

Join two of the 3" pieces with the red and white alternating. Make three more units just the same.

Cut four 3/4" x 2-1/4" red strips. Sew to each of the 2-1/4" units, with the colors alternating. Press. Add the navy squares to the left side of the 2-1/4" units. Press.

Make 4   Make 4

Sew the top parts of the flags to the bottom unit. Press.

Borders

Measure and cut the narrower border strips the *width* of the quilt. Measure and cut the wider borders the *length* of the quilt without borders. Set aside. Sew narrower border strips to the top and bottom of the quilt.

Add the flags to both ends of the remaining borders. Press. Add the side borders to the quilt. Press.

Quilting suggestions

Because of the large number of seams in the center of the quilt, simple quilting is best. By hand or machine, quilt a diagonal line running from the upper left-hand corner of each star block to the lower right hand corner. Or, machine stipple in the background areas. Quilt in the ditch around the inside of the body of the quilt. A motif or just parallel lines can be quilted in the border. A line of quilting around the navy square is all the quilting necessary in the flags, but you could also quilt in the ditch between every stripe in the flags.

Binding

Before binding, hand-baste a scant 1/4" from the edge of the quilt.

Sew the binding strip to the quilt with a 1/4" seam. (See page 12 for instructions on binding and mitered corners.) Trim the excess backing and batting even with the quilt top. Turn binding under 1/4", turn to the back side, covering the stitching line. Sew down by hand with matching thread.

STARS AND STRIPES

(20" x 22")

Cutting directions

CUT	TO YIELD

STARS

Background Fabric

4 - 1-1/2" strips	40 squares
	8 rectangles 1-1/2"x2-1/2"
	52 Easy Angle triangles*

Red Print Fabric

| 1 - 1-1/2" strip | 4 squares |
| | 16 Easy Angle triangles* |

Gold Print Fabric

| 1 - 1-1/2" strip | 4 squares |
| | 16 Easy Angle triangles* |

Navy Print Fabric

| 1 - 1-1/2" strip | 5 squares |
| | 20 Easy Angle triangles* |

*Layer background and colored fabrics right sides together and cut with Easy Angle. They will then be ready to chain sew.

NOTE: If not using Easy Angle, cut squares 1-7/8". Cut once on the diagonal.

FLAGS

Background Fabric for Flags

2 - 1" strips

Red Solid Fabric

3 - 1" strips

Navy Star Print Fabric

| 1 - 2" strip | 4 squares |

Tool Requirement
Easy Angle

Fabric Requirements
Background: 1/3 yard
Red print: 1/4 yard
Navy Star print for borders and flags: 1/2 yard
Scraps of navy print and gold print

BORDER AND BINDING
Navy Star Print Fabric

1 - 5-1/2" strip	2 - 5-1/2" x 11-1/2" (or length of the of the quilt)
1 - 4-1/2" strip	
	2 - 4" x 11-1/2" (or width of the center of the quilt)
3 - 1-1/4" strips	Binding

Flag assembly

Sew together one red and one background strip. Make two strip sets. Press toward the red fabric. Cut into eight units measuring 5-1/2", and four units measuring 4".

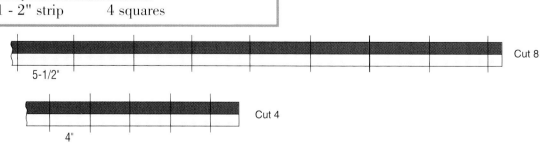

Cut 8

5-1/2"

Cut 4

4"

Join two 5-1/2" units for each flag. Press toward the red fabric.

Make 4   Make 4

Join the units to make four flags measuring 4" x 5-1/2" unfinished.

Make 4

Cut four 1" x 4" strips from the remaining red strip. Sew to the background side of the 4" unit. Press toward the red fabric. Sew a navy star square to the left side of this unit. Press toward the navy star.

Quilt assembly

Assemble the stars and finish the quilt according to the directions for the small **Stars and Stripes**.

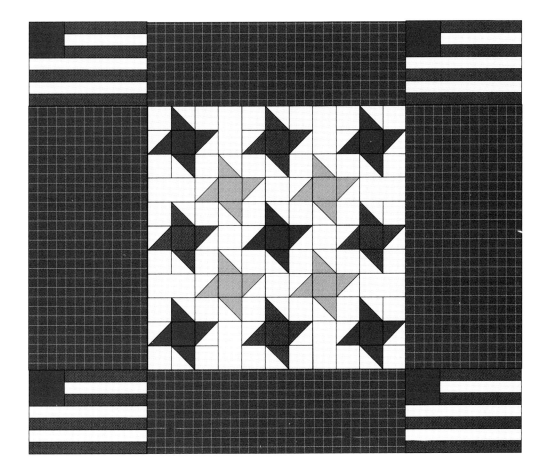

UNCLE SAM

(9-1/2" x 12-1/2")

What could be more Americana than Uncle Sam waving the U.S. flag? The inspiration for this quilt came from a primitive carving of Uncle Sam that leans more than a little to the left. Does this make him politically incorrect?

Tool Requirement
Easy Angle

Fabric Requirements
Scraps of red, white, navy, tan, beige background print, a striped blue and white or red and white fabric, and a navy fabric with white stars. Small amount of fusible webbing.

Optional Embellishments
Gold star or button
Small black bead or button for eye
Black embroidery floss or #8 pearl cotton

9-1/2" x 12-1/2"

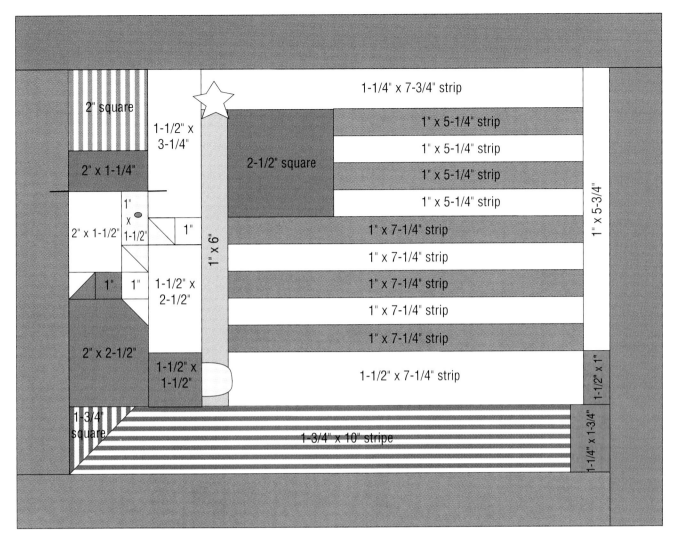

The diagram contains the following labels:

- 2" square
- 1-1/2" x 3-1/4"
- 1-1/4" x 7-3/4" strip
- 2" x 1-1/4"
- 2-1/2" square
- 1" x 5-1/4" strip
- 1" x 5-1/4" strip
- 1" x 5-1/4" strip
- 1" x 5-1/4" strip
- 1" x 1-1/2"
- 1"
- 2" x 1-1/2"
- 1" x 6"
- 1" x 7-1/4" strip
- 1" x 7-1/4" strip
- 1" x 7-1/4" strip
- 1" x 7-1/4" strip
- 1" x 5-3/4"
- 1"
- 1"
- 1-1/2" x 2-1/2"
- 1" x 7-1/4" strip
- 2" x 2-1/2"
- 1-1/2" x 1-1/2"
- 1-1/2" x 7-1/4" strip
- 1-1/2" x 1"
- 1-3/4" square
- 1-3/4" x 10" stripe
- 1-1/4" x 1-3/4"

Quilt assembly

Cut out the required pieces in the fabrics and sizes given in the diagram. The small triangle squares on Uncle Sam are cut from 1" strips of fabric using Easy Angle. (Or, cut 1-3/8" squares, cut once on the diagonal.) Sew, press, and trim dog ears on all the small triangle squares. Place a white 1" square on the upper right corner of the blue 2" x 2-1/2" rectangle. Stitch on the diagonal. Trim the seam allowance to 1/4" and press. Repeat this procedure for the 1-3/4" striped square.

Assemble the quilt in units. Join Uncle Sam to the background and flag units. Add his legs, then the borders. The borders are added in Log Cabin fashion, starting on the left side. First add the red left-handed border, then the bottom red border. Continue with the blue right-handed border, and finally the top blue border.

Fuse the hand in place over the flagpole.

Quilting suggestions

Quilt by hand or machine in the ditch around Uncle Sam, his beard, his jacket, hat, hand, pants and shoes. Quilt in the ditch around the flag and pole, around the star print square, and between each of the stripes in the flag. Also stitch in the ditch between the body of the quilt and the border.

Binding

Before binding, hand-baste a scant 1/4" away from the edge of the quilt.

Join the binding strips with diagonal seams pressed open and trimmed to 1/4". Sew the binding strips to the quilt with a 1/4" seam. (See page 12 for instructions on binding and mitered corners.) Trim the excess backing and batting even with the quilt top. Turn binding under 1/4", turn to the back side, covering the stitching line. Sew down by hand with matching thread.

Embellishment

Attach a black bead or button for Uncle Sam's eye. Add a star or round button to the top of the flagpole. Embroider the hat brim with two strands of black embroidery floss, extending the line 3/8" beyond the hat on either side.

Fall Quilts

SMALL BUTTERSCOTCH

(7-1/2" x 10-1/2", 2" block)

Tool Requirements
Easy Angle
Companion Angle

Fabric Requirements
Background:
  1/4 yard
Prints: Scraps of at
  least 6 different
  prints
Binding:
  1, 1-1/4" strip

Cutting directions

CUT	TO YIELD

Background Fabric

CUT	TO YIELD
1 - 2-1/2" strip	2 squares, 4 Easy Angle triangles for corners, 6 Companion Angle triangles for half blocks
4 - 1" strips	4 squares for pieced border corners
	24 squares for pieced blocks
	60 Easy Angle triangles for border*
	60 Easy Angle triangles for blocks*, 24 of which are "orphans"

Variety of Print Fabrics
(For each block cut) 2, 1-1/2" Easy Angle triangles

1" strip	6 Easy Angle triangles* and extras for border

Binding Fabric

CUT	TO YIELD
1 - 1-1/4" strip	Binding

*Layer background fabric and print fabric right sides together and cut with Easy Angle. They are then ready to chain sew.

NOTE: If not using Easy Angle, cut 1-3/8" and 1-7/8" squares for the blocks, and 2-7/8" squares for the large triangles. Cut once on the diagonal. If not using Companion Angle, cut 5-1/4" squares. Cut twice on the diagonal.

Block assembly

Assemble all the small triangle squares for each block. Press toward the darkest fabric. Trim "dog-ears." Assemble two small "four-patches" for each block.

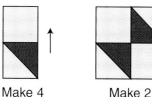

Make 4   Make 2

Add Easy Angle "orphans" to both sides of last two small triangle-squares. Press toward the "orphans."

Make 2

Add two pieced triangles to two large triangles to form two large triangle-squares. Press toward the large triangle.

Add the small four-patches to the large triangle-squares as shown. Press toward the large triangles.

Make 2

Make 1 from each fabric

Set the blocks together with plain blocks and half blocks on the diagonal. Join the diagonal rows. Add the last two corner triangles. Press.

Border

Assemble 60 triangle squares, using the prints from your blocks and any other prints you wish to add. Join 12 triangle squares for the top and bottom, having 6 of them pointing one direction, and 6 of them the other. Assemble 18 of them for the sides in the same manner. Press these borders, measure them, and then trim the quilt to the border measurements.

Add the top and bottom borders first. Press toward the quilt. Add the corner squares to both ends of the long borders. Sew the side borders to the quilt, again pressing toward the quilt.

Optional border

Instead of the pieced border, cut a 1-1/2" strip of one of your prints for the border.

Make 2 of each

Quilting suggestions

Hand quilt a pretty design in each of the plain blocks and a little "in the ditch" quilting in each block also. Or, machine stipple in all the setting blocks.

Binding

Before binding, hand-baste a scant 1/4" from the edge of your quilt. Sew the binding strip to the quilt with a 1/4" seam. (See page 12 for instructions on binding and mitered corners.) Trim the excess backing and batting. Turn binding under 1/4", turn to the back side, covering the stitching line. Sew down by hand with matching thread.

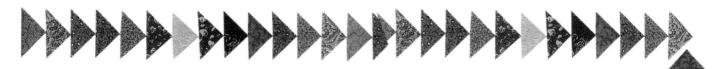

LARGE BUTTERSCOTCH

(20-1/2" x 26-1/2", 4" block)

Tool Requirements
Easy Angle
Companion Angle

Fabric Requirements
Green solid: 1 yard
Variety of '30s reproduction prints: scraps or fat quarters
Pink print: 1/4 yard for inside border

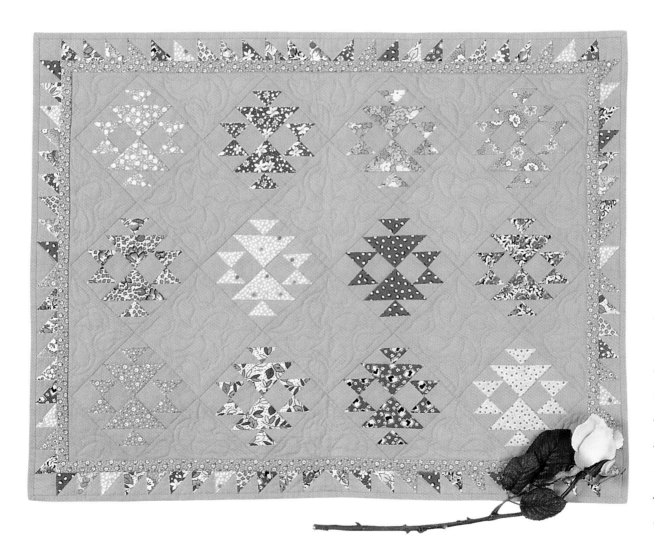

20-1/2" x 26-1/2"

Cutting directions

CUT	TO YIELD
Green Solid Fabric	
6 - 1-1/2" strips	48 squares
	120 Easy Angle triangles*
1 - 4-1/2" strip	6 squares for plain blocks
	2 squares cut diagonally
	(for corners)
2 - 4" strips	10 Companion Angles
	triangles (half blocks)
3 - 1-1/4" strips	Binding
Variety of Print Fabrics	
(For each block cut)	
1 - 2-1/2" strip	2 Easy Angle triangles
trim strip to 1-1/2"	6 Easy Angle triangles**
Pink Print Fabric	
3 - 1" strips	Inside border

*72 of these Easy Angle triangles are cut together with the triangles from the print fabrics. The other 48 triangles are "orphans."

**Layer background fabric and print fabric right sides together and cut triangles with Easy Angle. They will then be ready to chain-sew.

Optional sawtooth border

CUT	TO YIELD
Green Solid Fabric	
3 - 1-1/2" strips	84 Easy Angle triangles**
	4 squares
Variety of Print Fabrics	
1 - 1-1/2" strip	84 Easy Angle triangles**

NOTE: If not using Easy Angle, cut 1-7/8" squares for the small triangles, and 2-7/8" squares for the larger triangles. Cut once on the diagonal. If not using Companion Angle, cut three 8-1/4" squares. Cut twice on the diagonal.

Assembling the quilt

Assemble the blocks according to the diagrams in the **Small Butterscotch** pattern. Make 12 blocks.

Set the blocks together with plain blocks and half and corner blocks on the diagonal. Join the diagonal rows. Press the seams all one direction.

NOTE: The side and corner triangles are larger than needed and will be trimmed later.

Borders

Trim your quilt to 17-1/2" x 23-1/2". Cut top and bottom borders 1" x 17-1/2". Sew to the top and bottom of the quilt. Press toward the border.

Measure the *length* of the quilt. Cut two borders to this measurement and add to the sides of the quilt. Press toward the border.

Piece the sawtooth border, reversing the direction of the "teeth" in the middle of each border. Assemble 18 "teeth" for the top and bottom borders, and 24 "teeth" for the side borders. You can adjust the inside border to the measurements of the pieced border if necessary.

Quilting suggestions

If you enjoy hand quilting, this quilt gives you the opportunity to showcase your quilting in the plain blocks. In the pieced blocks, by hand or machine, quilt in the ditch or 1/4" from the seam in the large triangles. Stitch in the ditch around each of the smaller triangles and around each of the blocks. Stitch in the ditch on both sides of the inside border and around each of the triangles in the pieced border.

If you prefer quilting by machine, stitch in the ditch on all the diagonal lines and in the large "bowtie" in the center of the blocks. Quilt a pretty design in the plain blocks and half blocks. Quilt in the ditch on both sides of the narrow border and around each of the triangles in the border.

Binding

Before binding, hand baste a scant 1/4" from the edge of the quilt.

Join the binding strips with diagonal seams pressed open and trimmed to 1/4". Sew the binding strips to the quilt with a 1/4" seam. (See page 12 for instructions on binding and mitered corners.) Trim the excess backing and batting even with the quilt top. Turn binding under 1/4", turn to the back side, covering the stitching line. Sew down by hand with matching thread.

SMALL CHURN DASH

(14-3/4" square, 1-1/2" block)

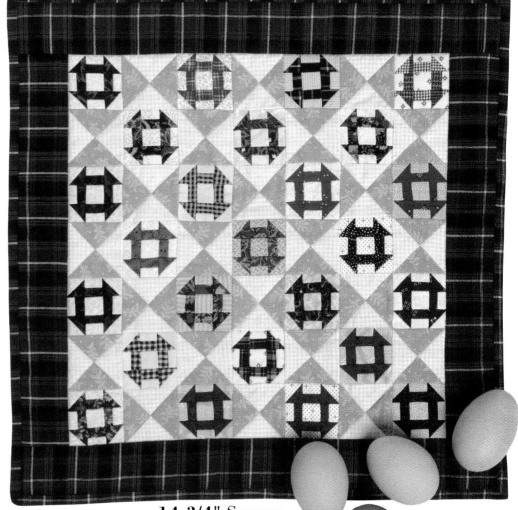

Can you find the hidden stars in the quilt? The stars are formed by the setting blocks. These charming 1-1/2" Churn Dash blocks are made from a variety of background fabrics and dark prints and plaids. If you use different fabrics in every one of the twenty-five Churn Dash blocks, you will have a charm quilt.

14-3/4" Square

Tool Requirements

Easy Angle   Companion Angle

Fabric Requirements

For 25 Churn Dash blocks: Scraps in a variety of background fabrics and scraps of prints in dark blues, browns, blacks and reds. You will need one 1" x 11" strip each of background and print for each Churn Dash block. (Use a 1-3/8" strip if not using Easy Angle.)

For the 24 setting blocks: Two shades of background, a light tan and a dark tan; two 1-1/4" strips of each. (If not using Companion Angle, cut 12 2-3/4" squares from both fabrics, cut twice on the diagonal.)

For the border and binding, you need 1/4 yard of a dark plaid or print.

Cutting and assembly directions

For each Churn Dash block, cut:

One 1" square of background for center; then layer the background and print 1" fabric strips right sides together and cut four pairs of Easy Angle triangles. Sew the Easy Angle triangles. Press toward the darker fabric. Trim "dog-ears."

Make 4

Trim the remainder of the strips down to 3/4".

Join the two strips with a 1/4" seam. Press to the light fabric and re-cut into four 1" squares.

Cut into 4, 1" squares

Assemble the Churn Dash block as shown.

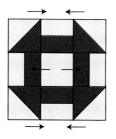

Make 25

Assembling the setting blocks

Layer 1-1/4" dark and light background fabric strips right sides together, and cut 48 pairs of triangles with Companion Angle. Sew all the triangles on the right side with the lightest triangle on top. Press toward the dark triangle.

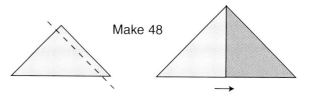

Make 48

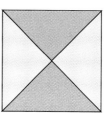

Join two sets of triangles to make the setting block. Press.

Assemble the quilt as shown in the diagram, turning the setting blocks to achieve the "hidden stars" effect.

Make 24

Borders

Cut two 2" strips of the border fabric. Measure and cut two borders the *width* of the quilt. Sew to the top and bottom of the quilt. Press the seams toward the border.

Measure and cut two border strips the *length* of the quilt. Sew to the sides of the quilt. Press the seams toward the border.

Quilting suggestions

Quilt in the ditch by machine or by hand on the diagonal lines and the inside edge of the body of the quilt.

Binding

Before binding, hand-baste a scant 1/4" from the edge of the quilt.

Cut two binding strips 1-1/4" wide. Join the binding strips with diagonal seams pressed open and trimmed to 1/4". Sew the binding strips to the quilt with a 1/4" seam. (See page 12 for instructions on binding and mitered corners.) Trim the excess backing and batting even with the quilt top. Turn binding under 1/4", turn to the back side, covering the stitching line. Sew down by hand with matching thread.

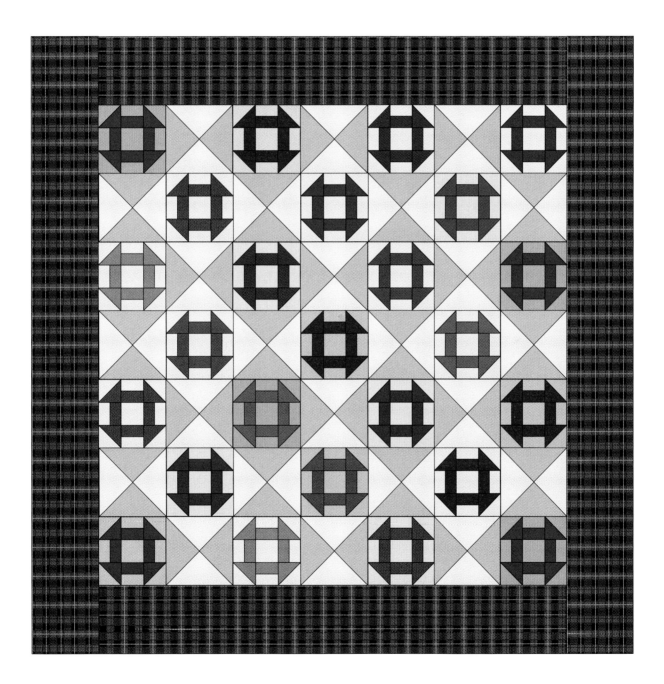

LARGE CHURN DASH

(17" x 20", 3" blocks)

A lovely border print was the inspiration for this quilt. A larger version of the Churn Dash block was used, and this quilt is set with sashing for a totally different look. A variety of red prints were used for each of the Churn Dash blocks to give the quilt a scrappy yet elegant look.

Tool Requirement
Easy Angle

Fabric Requirements
Background: 1/4 yard
Variety of red prints: scraps
Navy solid for sashing and binding: 1/4 yard
Medium brown print (for corner stones): scraps
Border print: 1/4 yard

17" x 20"

Cutting directions

CUT	TO YIELD
Background Fabric	
2 - 1-1/2" strips	12 squares
	48 Easy Angle triangles*
2 - 1" strips	
Red Print Fabrics	
1 - 1-1/2" x 12" strip from **each** red print	
Navy Solid Fabric	
3 - 1" strips	17 sashing strips 1" x 3-1/2"
	Inside border
2 - 1-1/4" strips	Binding
Medium Brown Fabric	
	6 - 1" squares for stepping-stones
Border Print Fabric	
2 - 3-1/4" strips	Outside border

*Lay red and background fabrics right sides together and cut with Easy Angle. They will then be ready to chain sew.

NOTE: If not using Easy Angle, cut 1-7/8" squares. Cut once on the diagonal.

Block assembly

Layer each 1-1/2" x 12" red strip right sides together with the 1-1/2" background strip and cut four pairs of Easy Angle triangles. Sew and press the seams toward the red print. Trim "dog ears."

Make 4

Cut into 4, 1-1/2" squares

Cut the remainder of the red strip to 1". Lay right sides together with the 1" background strip and sew. Press toward the red strip. Cut into four 1-1/2" squares for **each** block.

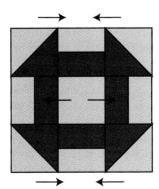

With the triangle squares, the two color squares, and a background center square, assemble the Churn Dash blocks. Press as directed.

Make 12 blocks

Quilt assembly

When all the Churn Dash blocks are completed, add the sashing strips and corner stones between the blocks. (NOTE: Be careful to align the points on the Churn Dash blocks with the points of the adjoining blocks.) Press seams toward the sashings.

Add inside and outside borders.

Quilting suggestions

By hand or machine, stitch in the ditch around each block, and also around the inside squares in each Churn Dash. Quilt in the ditch between the borders. A design can be quilted in the outside border, or just follow the design lines in the border print.

Binding

Before binding, hand-baste a scant 1/4" from the edge of your quilt.

Join the binding strips with diagonal seams pressed open and trimmed to 1/4". Sew the binding strips to the quilt with a 1/4" seam. (See page 12 for instructions on binding and mitered corners.) Trim the excess backing and batting even with the quilt top. Turn binding under 1/4", turn to the back side, covering the stitching line. Sew down by hand with matching thread.

SMALL HOME SWEET HOME

(12" square, 2" blocks)

Home is a cozy cabin in the woods, surrounded by trees with stars overheard. A light is shining in the window—someone is waiting for you to come home.

Tool Requirements
Easy Angle
Companion Angle

Fabric Requirements
Background: 1/4 yard
Green plaid: 1/4 yard

You need scraps of dark green for the trees, an assortment of dark brown fabrics for the cabin, tree trunks and corner stones, gold for the stars, window, sashing and inside border, and red for the cabin door and roof peak.

12" Square

Cutting directions for small Home Sweet Home

CUT	TO YIELD

STARS
Background Fabric
1 - 1" strip   16 squares
            16 Companion Angle triangles

Gold Fabric
(For *each* star cut)
1 - 1-1/2" square
1 - 1" strip   8 Easy Angle triangles

TREES
Background Fabric
2 - 1" strips   8 - 1" x 1-1/2" rectangles
            16 - 1" x 1-3/4" rectangles
            8 - 1" x 2" rectangles

Green Fabric
(For *each* tree cut)
1" strip   1 - 1" x 1-1/2" rectangle
          1 - 1" x 2-1/2" rectangle
          1 - 1" x 2-1/2" rectangle

Brown Fabric (trunks)
          4 - 1" x 3/4" rectangles

CABIN
Background Fabric
1 - 1" strip   2 Easy Angle triangles
          1" x 2-1/2" rectangle
          (above cabin)

Green Fabric
1 - 1" strip   1 - 1" x 2-1/2" rectangle
          (below cabin)

Gold Fabric (window)
          3/4" square

Brown Fabric
          3/4" strips of assorted browns
Roof piece cut from 1" strip, cut first angle with
Easy Angle, measure 1-1/2" at the base, and
cut again

Red Fabric (door and roof peak)
1 - 1" strip   1" Companion Angle triangle
          1"x 3/4" rectangle

SASHES AND BORDERS
Brown Fabric
1 - 1" strip   8 - 1" squares for cornerstones
Gold Fabric
2 - 1" strips   12 - 1" x 2-1/2" sashes
          Inside border
Green Plaid Fabric
1 - 2-1/2" strip   Outside border
2 - 1-1/4" strips   Binding

NOTE: If not using Easy Angle, cut 1-3/8"
squares. Cut once on the diagonal.
     If not using Companion Angle, cut 2-1/4"
squares, cut twice on the diagonal.

Star block assembly

Add the small gold triangles to both sides of the larger background triangle, making "flying geese" units. Press.

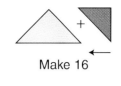

Make 16

Make 16

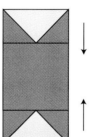

Make 4

Sew two flying geese units to opposite sides of the gold square. Press toward the square.

Add the background squares to both ends of the remaining geese units. Press toward the squares.

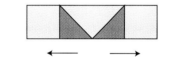

Make 8

Join the three units to form a star. Press toward the large square.

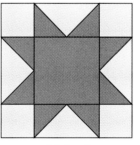

Make 4

Log Cabin block assembly

Assemble the front of the cabin by adding 3/4" strips to the red door. The strips are added in the manner of constructing a Log Cabin block.

Assemble the side of the cabin by adding strips to the window in the same manner as the front of the cabin.

Sew the red roof peak to the brown roof. Add the background triangles to both sides of the roof.

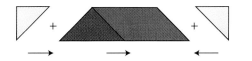

Join the two pieces of the cabin. Press. Add the roof strip. Press. Add the 1" strip of background above the cabin, and the green strip below the cabin. Trim the entire block to 2-1/2" square.

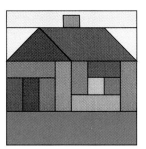

Tree block assembly

Mark a diagonal line on one corner of the background rectangles. Sew on the marked line, trim to 1/4", and press toward the green. Continue in this manner.

The 1" x 1-1/2" background rectangles are sewn to the 1" x 2-1/2" green rectangles.

The 1" x 1-3/4" background rectangles are sewn to the 1" x 2" green rectangles.

The 1" x 2" background rectangles are sewn to the 1" x 1-1/2" green rectangles.

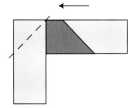

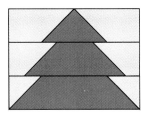

Make 4

Join the rows by creasing each "branch" in the center and matching the centers. Press the branches toward the bottom of the tree.

Sew the 1" x 1-3/4" background rectangles to both sides of the trunks. Press toward the trunks. Add the trunk strips to the bottom of the trees, centering the trunk. Press the seams toward the trees. Trim the finished tree blocks to 2-1/2" square.

Quilt assembly

Lay out the finished blocks with the stars in the corners, the trees in between, and the cabin in the center. Add sashings between the blocks and corner stones in the sashing.

Borders

To add an inside border of sashing fabric, measure and cut four borders the exact measurement of the quilt. Sew the top and bottom borders to the quilt. Press the seams toward the sashing.

Sew the cornerstones to both ends of the remaining borders. Press toward the border fabric. Sew to the sides of the quilt. Press the seams toward the border.

Measure and cut two outside borders the *width* of the quilt. Sew to the top and bottom of the quilt. Press the seams toward the border. Measure and cut two side borders the exact *length* of the quilt. Sew to the sides of the quilt. Press the seams toward the border.

Embellishments

A small chimney can be added with embroidery floss in satin stitch.

Quilting suggestions

The individual pieces in the blocks are so small you may chose to just quilt in the ditch inside each of the blocks and between the two borders.

Binding

Before binding, hand-baste a scant 1/4" from the edge of the quilt.

Join the binding strips with diagonal seams pressed open and trimmed to 1/4". Sew the binding strips to the quilt with a 1/4" seam. (See page 12 for instructions on binding and mitered corners.) Trim the excess backing and batting even with the quilt top. Turn binding under 1/4", turn to the back side, covering the stitching line. Sew down by hand with matching thread.

LARGE HOME SWEET HOME

(20" square, 4" block)

Tool Requirements
Easy Angle
Companion Angle

Fabric Requirements
Background: 1/3 yard
Medium brown: 1/3 yard
Green plaid: 1/4 yard
Scraps of green, brown, red, and gold

20" Square

Cutting directions large Home Sweet Home

CUT	TO YIELD

STARS

Background Fabric

2 - 1-1/2" strips — 16 squares
16 Companion Angle triangles

Gold Fabric

(For *each* star cut)

1 - 1-1/2" strip — 8 Easy Angle triangles
1 - 2-1/2" strip — 1 square for star center

TREES

Background Fabric

3 - 1-1/2" strips — 8 - 1-1/2" x 2" rectangles
8 - 1-1/2" x 2-1/2" rectangles
8 - 1-1/2" x 3" rectangles
8 - 1-1/2" x 2-3/4" rectangles
for trunk strip

Green Fabric

2 - 1-1/2" strips — 4 - 1-1/2" x 2-1/2" rectangles
4 - 1/1/2" x 3-1/2" rectangles
4 - 1-1/2" x 4-1/2" rectangles

Brown Fabric

1 - 1-1/2" strip — 4 - 1" x 1-1/2" rectangles

CABIN

Brown Fabric

1" strips of assorted brown prints for cabin

Red Fabric

1 - 1-1/2" strip — 1 Companion Angle triangle (roof peak)
1" x 1-1/2" rectangle (door)

Gold Fabric

1 - 1" square (window)

Background Fabric

1 - 1-1/2" strip — 2 Easy Angle triangles
1 - 1-1/2" x 4-1/2" rectangle (above cabin)

Green Fabric

1 - 1-1/2" strip — 1 - 1-1/2" x 4-1/2" rectangle (below cabin)

SASHING AND BORDERS

Brown Fabric

4 - 1" squares for corner stones

Medium Brown Fabric

3 - 1" strips — 12 - 1" x 4-1/2" sashes
Inside border

3 - 1-1/4" strips — Binding

Green Plaid Fabric

2 - 3" strips — Outside border

NOTE: If not using Easy Angle, cut 1-7/8" squares. Cut once on the diagonal.

If not using Companion Angle, cut 3-1/4" squares. Cut twice on the diagonal.

Block assembly

Assemble each of the blocks according to the directions for the smaller *Home Sweet Home* quilt. For the tree blocks, sew:

1-1/2" x 2" background rectangles to 1-1/2" x 4-1/2" green rectangles

1-1/2" x 2-1/2" background rectangles to 1-1/2" x 3-1/2" green rectangles

1-1/2" x 3" background rectangles to 1-1/2" x 2-1/2" green rectangles

1-1/2" x 2-3/4" background rectangles to 1-1/2" x 1" brown rectangles

The tree blocks are trimmed to 4-1/2".

The roof piece is cut from a 1-1/2" strip of brown. Cut the first angle with Easy Angle, measure 2-3/4" at the base, and cut again with Easy Angle.

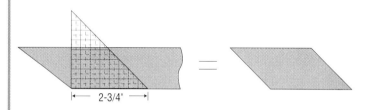

Quilt assembly and finishing

Assemble the quilt following the directions for the smaller size. Quilt and bind.

SMALL MAPLE LEAF JAZZ

(12-1/2" x 14-3/4", 1-1/2" block)

The leaf print used for the border of this quilt is not typical leaf colors. I thought the hot pink leaves added a little "jazz" to a traditional pattern, hence the name "Maple Leaf Jazz."

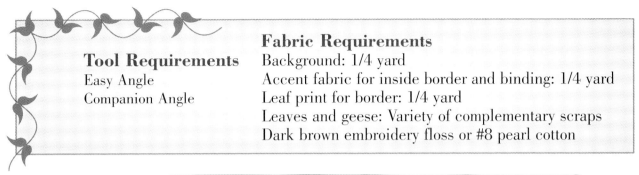

Tool Requirements
Easy Angle
Companion Angle

Fabric Requirements
Background: 1/4 yard
Accent fabric for inside border and binding: 1/4 yard
Leaf print for border: 1/4 yard
Leaves and geese: Variety of complementary scraps
Dark brown embroidery floss or #8 pearl cotton

12-1/2" x 14-3/4"

Cutting directions

CUT	TO YIELD

MAPLE LEAVES
Background Fabric

3 - 1" strips	24 squares
	48 Easy Angle triangles*

Twelve Print Fabrics
From *each* of 12 prints

1" x 7" strip	3 squares
	4 Easy Angle triangles*

*Layer background and print strips right sides together before cutting triangles. They will then be ready to chain sew.

FLYING GEESE
Background Fabric

2 - 1" strips	60 Easy Angle triangles

Variety of Print Fabrics

1" strips	30 Companion Angle triangles

NOTE: If not using Easy Angle, cut 1-3/8" squares. Cut once on the diagonal.

If not using Companion Angle, cut 2-1/4" squares. Cut twice on the diagonal.

SASHINGS AND BORDERS
Background Fabric

2 - 1" strips	9 sashing strips 1" x 2"
	6 spacing strips 1" x 8"

Accent Fabric

1 - 1" strip	Inside border
2 - 1-1/4" strips	Binding

Leaf Print Fabric

2 - 2-1/2" strips	Outside border

Assembling the Maple-Leaf blocks

Assemble all the triangle squares you have cut for the Maple Leaf blocks. Press toward the print fabric. Trim dog-ears. Assemble each leaf in rows.

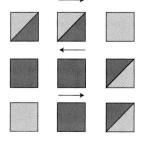

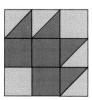

Make 12

Press, following directional arrows. Join the three rows, then press again. (***NOTE:*** Add the embroidered stem after the entire top is assembled and borders are added.)

Add the 1" x 2" sashing strips between the Maple Leaves, joining four leaves in three rows. Press the seams toward the sashing strips.

Assembling the flying geese

To assemble all the geese units, begin by sewing a background triangle to the right side of each of the goose triangles. Press toward the darker fabric.

Make 30

Add the second background triangle on the left side. Press toward the background triangle. Trim dog-ears.

Make 30

Assembling the quilt

Assemble all of the geese in rows of 15. Press. (***NOTE:*** The length of these rows should equal the length of the Maple Leaf strip. If not, slight adjustments can be made in the sashing strips on the Maple Leaf row.)

Add the 1" background spacer strips between the rows of leaves and the flying geese. You may change the direction of your geese or leaves as you wish. (The debate rages on as to which direction the leaves should go: pointing up or falling down. You decide—it's your quilt!) Also add spacer strips on the top and bottom of the quilt to make it more rectangular.

116

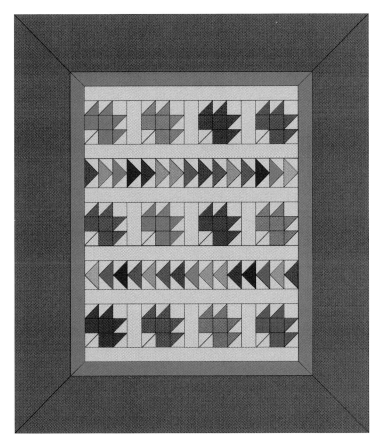

Embellishment

Before quilting, add stems to the leaves with two strands of embroidery floss or one strand of pearl cotton using an outline stitch or just one large stitch. Or, simply mark the stem with a Pigma marker.

Quilting suggestions

By hand or by machine, quilt in the ditch around each of the Maple Leaf blocks and on both sides of the flying geese strip. Or, machine quilt a small meander in all the background areas. This will fill the background nicely without interfering with the design. Also, stitch in the ditch on both sides of the inside border. Quilt a simple design in the border if you wish.

Binding

Before quilting, hand-baste a scant 1/4" from the edge of the quilt.

Join the binding strips with diagonal seams pressed open and trimmed to 1/4". Sew the binding strips to the quilt with a 1/4" seam. (See page 12 for instructions on binding and mitered corners.) Trim the excess backing and batting even with the quilt top. Turn binding under 1/4", turn to the back side, covering the stitching line. Sew down by hand with matching thread.

Borders

Measure the *width* of the quilt and cut two narrow borders to this measurement. Sew to the top and bottom of the quilt. Press the seams toward the border.

Measure the *length* of the quilt and cut two narrow borders to this measurement. Sew to the top and bottom of the quilt. Press the seams toward the border.

Repeat this procedure for the wider leaf print borders.

LARGE
MAPLE LEAF JAZZ

(20-1/2" x 24-1/2", 3" block)

Tool Requirements
Easy Angle
Companion Angle

Fabric Requirements
Background: 1/2 yard
Border and binding: 1/3 yard
Accent for inside border: 1/8 yard
Scraps in various coordinating colors for leaves
and geese.

Cutting directions

CUT	TO YIELD
MAPLE LEAVES	
Background Fabric	
1 - 1-1/2" strip	24 squares
2 - 1-1/2" strips	48 Easy Angle triangles*
Print Fabrics	
From *each* print	
1-1/2" x 10" strip	3 squares
	4 Easy Angle triangles*

*Layer background and print strips right sides together and cut. They will then be ready to chain sew.

FLYING GEESE	
Variety of Print Fabrics	
1-1/2" strips	30 Companion Angle triangles
Background Fabric	
2 - 1-1/2" strips	60 Easy Angle triangles

SASHINGS AND BORDERS	
Background Fabric	
4 - 1-1/2" strips	9 sashing strips 1-1/2" x 3-1/2"
	6 spacing strips
	1-1/2" x 15-1/2"
Accent Fabric	
2 - 1" strips	Inside border
Leaf Print Fabric	
2 - 3" strips	Outside border
3 - 1-1/4" strips	Binding

NOTE: If not using Easy Angle, cut 1-7/8" squares. Cut once on the diagonal.
If not using Companion Angle, cut 3-1/4" squares. Cut twice on the diagonal.

20-1/2" x 24-1/2"

Quilt assembly and finishing

Assemble the units and quilt top using the directions from the small *Maple Leaf Jazz* pattern.

Quilt and finish in the same manner as the smaller quilt.

MY HEART IS IN MINNESOTA
SMALL SAMPLER (14-1/2" x 17")

Take all your favorite blocks from this book, add your best scraps, and mix them together. The result will be this wonderful sampler.

Tool Requirements
Easy Angle
Companion Angle

Fabric Requirements
A large variety of scraps in red, brown, green, gold, navy and black, and a number of background fabrics in tan and beige.
Border: 1/4 yard
Fusible webbing: 1/4 yard
Embroidery Floss or #8 pearl cotton in brown or black

14-1/2" x 17"

Cutting and assembling the quilt

You will find directions for all of the blocks (except the cabin) in other patterns in this book. Please refer to those pages for cutting and assembling directions. The illustration for the *Minnesota Sampler* will tell you the sizes to cut of the spacer strips. The pattern for the cabin is given at right.

You need:
6 trees, (*trimmed to the sizes indicated on the graphic*) from *Home Sweet Home*
6 Maple Leaves
3 Friendship Stars (from *Stars and Stripes*)
1 Bear's Paw block (from *Miniature Bear's Paw*)
1 Single Wedding Ring block
3 Churn Dash blocks
1 Butterscotch block
25 Flying Geese units (from *Maple Leaf Jazz*)
2 Sawtooth Stars (from *Scrappy Delight*)
1 Flag (from *Stars and Stripes*)
2 hearts, cut from templates

Log Cabin

Cut 1" logs from a variety of brown prints. Cut a door from red fabric 1" x 1-1/2". Cut a 1" square from gold fabric for the window.

Beginning with the door for the front portion of the house, begin adding "logs" using the method for assembling a Log Cabin block, following the numbered sequence on the diagram.

Assemble the window side of the house in the same manner, following the numbered sequence on the diagram.

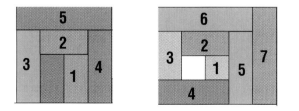

For the roof, cut a 1-1/2" strip of black print. Cut the left side of the roof angle with Easy Angle. Measure across the base 3-1/4", and cut the roof angle again with your Easy Angle.

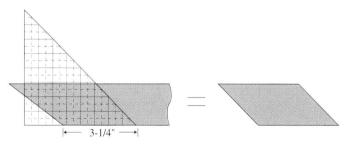

For the roof peak, cut a strip 1-1/2" wide, and, using Companion Angle, cut one triangle.

From a background fabric, cut a strip 1-1/2" wide, then cut two Easy Angle triangles from that strip. Assemble the roof unit. Press.

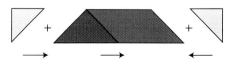

The chimney is a 1" square of red fabric. Add the background strips as indicated on the diagram. When finished, the Log Cabin unit should measure 4-1/2" x 6" including the seam allowances and side spacer strips.

NOTE: If not using Easy Angle, cut 1-7/8" squares. Cut once on the diagonal.

If not using Companion Angle, cut a 3-1/4" square. Cut twice on the diagonal.

Butterscotch block

Cut a 2-1/4" strip of background fabric. Cut four Easy Angle triangles. Add to all four sides of the small *Butterscotch* block. Press. Trim the square to 3-1/2", leaving 1/4" seam allowances on all four sides.

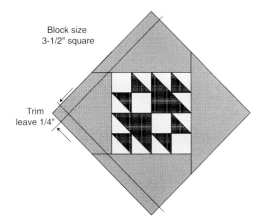

Block size
3-1/2" square

Trim
leave 1/4"

NOTE: If not using Easy Angle, cut 2-5/8" squares. Cut once on the diagonal.

Flag block

Assemble one flag according to the directions in the small *Stars and Stripes* pattern. Remove the bottom red strip.

Quilt assembly

Assemble all the units in sections as indicated with darker lines in the diagram.

Join all the sections.

Borders

Cut borders 2" wide. Measure and cut two borders the exact *width* of the quilt. Sew to the top and bottom of the quilt. Press the seams toward the border.

Measure and cut two borders the exact *length* of the quilt. Sew to the sides of the quilt. Press the seams toward the border.

Embellishment

Fuse the two hearts onto the two plain blocks. Embroider the maple leaf stems with two strands of black or brown embroidery floss.

Large Heart Template   Small Heart Template

Quilting suggestions

There are a large number of seams and tiny pieces in this sampler, so quilt (by hand or machine) only in the ditch around each of the blocks and around the inside of the border. A few lines in the ditch around the Log Cabin and around the hearts may be added if you wish.

Binding

Before binding, hand baste a scant 1/4" from the edge of the quilt.

Using a dark fabric, cut two strips 1-1/4" wide on the straight-of-grain for a single, narrow binding.

Join the binding strips with diagonal seams pressed open and trimmed to 1/4". Sew the binding strips to the quilt with a 1/4" seam. (See page 12 for instructions on binding and mitered corners.) Trim the excess backing and batting even with the quilt top. Turn binding under 1/4", turn to the back side, covering the stitching line. Sew down by hand with matching thread.

LARGE MINNESOTA SAMPLER

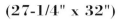

(27-1/4" x 32")

Tool Requirements
Easy Angle
Companion Angle

Fabric Requirements
A large variety of scraps in red, brown, green, gold, navy and black, and a number of background fabrics in tan and beige
Border and Binding: 1/2 yard

The large **Minnesota Sampler** is the same as the smaller version, but the pieces are cut from 1-1/2" strips instead of 1" strips. Please refer to the directions for the smaller quilt and the illustration below for the sizes of the spacer strips and blocks.

Follow the directions for the smaller version, but make the large block sizes for each pattern in the required numbers.

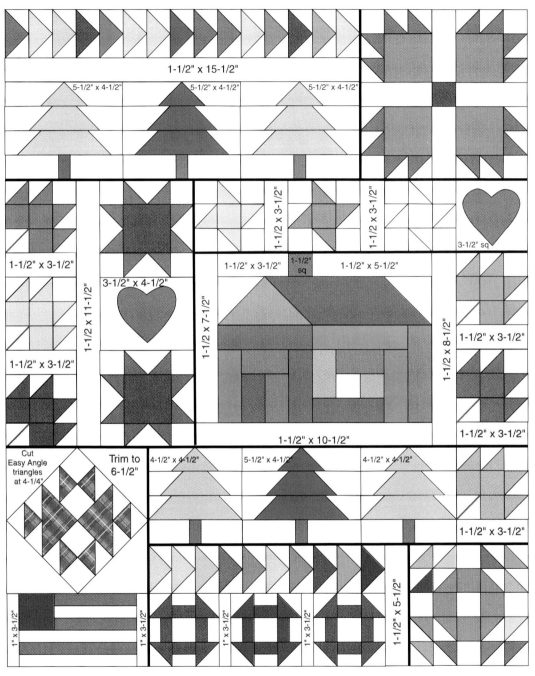

Log Cabin

Cut 1-1/2" logs from a variety of brown prints. Cut a door from red fabric 1-1/2" x 2-1/2". Cut a 1-1/2" square from gold fabric for the window.

Beginning with the door for the front portion of the house, begin adding "logs" using the same method for assembling a Log Cabin block, following the numbered sequence on the diagram.

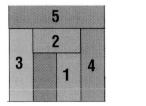
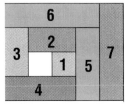

Assemble the window side of the house in the same manner, following the numbered sequence on the diagram.

For the roof, cut a 2-1/2" strip of black print. Cut the left side of the roof angle with Easy Angle. Measure across the base 5-3/4", and cut the roof angle again with your Easy Angle.

For the roof peak, cut a strip 2-1/2" wide, and, using Companion Angle, cut one triangle.

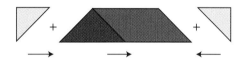

From a background fabric, cut a strip 2-1/2"wide, then cut two Easy Angle triangles from that strip. Assemble the roof unit. Press.

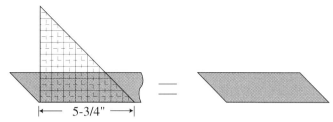

The chimney is a 1-1/2" square of red fabric. Add the background strips as indicated on the diagram. When finished, the Log Cabin unit should measure 8-1/2" x 11-1/2" including the seam allowances and the side and bottom spacer strips.

NOTE: If not using Easy Angle, cut 2-7/8" squares. Cut once on the diagonal.

If not using Companion Angle, cut a 5-1/4" square. Cut twice on the diagonal.

Butterscotch block

Cut a 4-1/4" strip of background fabric. Cut four Easy Angle triangles. Add to all four sides of the Butterscotch block. Press. Trim the square to 6-1/2", leaving 1/4" seam allowances on all four sides.

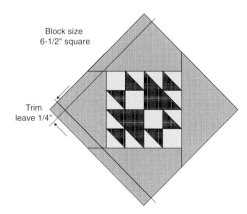

Block size
6-1/2" square

Trim
leave 1/4"

NOTE: If not using Easy Angle, cut 4-5/8" squares. Cut once on the diagonal.

Flag block

Make one flag according to the directions in **Large Stars and Stripes**. Remove the last red strip at the bottom of the flag.

Quilt assembly

Assemble all the units in sections as indicated with darker lines in the diagram.

Assemble all the sections.

Borders

Cut borders 3" wide. Measure and cut two borders the exact *width* of the quilt. Sew to the top and bottom of the quilt. Press the seams toward the borders.

Measure and cut two borders the exact *length* of the quilt. Sew to the sides of the quilt. Press the seams toward the borders.

Follow the quilting and finishing directions for **My Heart is in Minnesota Sampler—Small.**

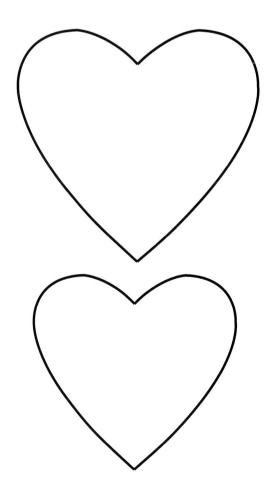

PINE TREE RIDGE

(16" square, 2" blocks)

Tool Requirements	Fabric Requirements
Easy Angle	Background: 1/4 yard
Companion Angle	4 Assorted green prints: 1/4 yard total (at least 1/6 yard of one green print)
	Gold: 1/8 yard
	Red print: 1/8 yard
	Brown: scraps
	Black: 1/4 yard

16" square

Cutting directions for trees

CUT	TO YIELD
Background Fabric	
5 - 1" strips	24 - 1" x 1-1/2" rectangles
	48 - 1" x 1-3/4" rectangles
	24 - 1" x 2"
4 Green Fabrics	
From *each* green	
1 - 1" strip	3 - 1" x 1-1/2" rectangles
	3 - 1" x 2" rectangles
	3 - 1" x 2-1/2" rectangles
Brown Fabric	
1 - 1" strip	12 1" x 3/4" rectangles

Cutting directions for stars

CUT	TO YIELD
Background Fabric	
2 - 1" strips	52 Companion Angle triangles
Gold Fabric	
3 - 1" strips	104 Easy Angle triangles
Red Fabric	
1 - 1-1/2" strip	13 - 1-1/2" squares
2 - 1" strips	52 - 1" squares

NOTE: If not using Easy Angle, cut 1-3/8" squares. Cut once on the diagonal.

If not using Companion Angle, cut 2-1/4" squares. Cut twice on the diagonal.

Tree block assembly

Mark a diagonal line on one corner of the background rectangle as shown in the diagram. Sew the background rectangles to both sides of the green rectangles on the marked line, trim to 1/4", and press toward the green rectangle.

Match up the rectangles as follows:

1" x 1-1/2" background rectangles to the 1" x 2-1/2" green rectangles.

1" x 1-3/4" background rectangles to the 1" x 2" green rectangles.

1" x 2" background rectangles to the 1" x 1-1/2" green rectangles.

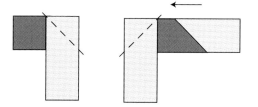

Join the rows by creasing each "branch" in the center and matching the centers. Press the branches toward the bottom of the tree. Make 12 trees.

Sew the 1" x 1-3/4" background rectangles to both sides of the trunks. Press toward the trunk. Add the trunk strip to the bottom of the trees, centering the trunk. Press the seams toward the trees. Trim the finished tree blocks to 2-1/2" square.

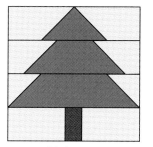

Make 12

Star block assembly

Add the small gold triangles to both sides of the larger background triangle, making "flying geese"

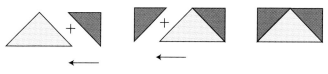

Make 52   Make 52

units. Press.

Sew two flying geese units to opposite sides of the large square. Press toward the square.

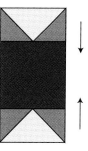

Make 13

Add the small squares to both sides of the remaining flying geese units. Press toward the small squares.

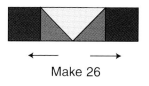

Make 26

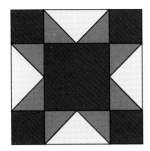

Join the three units to form a star. Press toward the large square.

Make 13

Quilt assembly

Alternate the star and tree blocks in five rows of five blocks each. Sew the blocks together in horizontal rows. Press the seams toward the tree blocks.

Join the horizontal rows. Press the seams all one direction.

Cutting directions for borders

CUT	TO YIELD
Black Fabric	
2 - 1" strips	Inside border
2 - 1-1/4" strips	Binding
Green Fabric	
2 - 2-1/2" strips	Outside border

Borders

Measure and cut two narrow border strips the *width* of the quilt top. Sew to the top and bottom of the quilt. Press toward the borders.

Measure and cut two narrow border strips to the *length* of the quilt. Sew to the sides of the quilt and press toward the borders.

Measure and cut the wider borders in the same manner. Sew to the quilt. Press the seams toward the borders.

Quilting suggestions

Quilt diagonal lines running through the stars. Quilt inside and outside the first narrow border. Quilt a design in the wider outer border.

Binding

Before binding, hand-baste a scant 1/4" from the edge of the quilt.

Join the binding strips with diagonal seams pressed open and trimmed to 1/4". Sew the binding strips to the quilt with a 1/4" seam. (See page 12 for instructions on binding and mitered corners.) Trim the excess backing and batting even with the quilt top. Turn binding under 1/4", turn to the back side, covering the stitching line. Sew down by hand with matching thread.